Workshop on Computational Approaches to Causality in Language 2014

Held at the 14th Conference of the European Chapter of the Association for Computer Linguistics

Gothenburg, Sweden
26 April 2014

ISBN: 978-1-63266-402-0

Printed from e-media with permission by:

Curran Associates, Inc.
57 Morehouse Lane
Red Hook, NY 12571

Some format issues inherent in the e-media version may also appear in this print version.

Printed by Curran Associates, Inc. (2014)

For permission requests, please contact the Association for Computational Linguistics at the address below.

Association for Computational Linguistics
209 N. Eighth Street
Stroudsburg, Pennsylvania 18360

Phone: 1-570-476-8006
Fax: 1-570-476-0860

acl@aclweb.org

Additional copies of this publication are available from:

Curran Associates, Inc.
57 Morehouse Lane
Red Hook, NY 12571 USA
Phone: 845-758-0400
Fax: 845-758-2634
Email: curran@proceedings.com
Web: www.proceedings.com

EACL 2014

14th Conference of the European Chapter of the Association for Computational Linguistics

Proceedings of the Workshop on Computational Approaches to Causality in Language

April 26, 2014
Gothenburg, Sweden

Supported by:

MUSE Machine Understanding for interactive StorytElling, EU FP7-296703

Preface

Causality is a research field with roots in philosophy, psychology, physics and application domains in medicine and knowledge engineering. It focuses on cause-effect, or causal, relations between two events or actions, in which one (the cause), causes the other (the effect). This information can be used in a number of natural language processing applications such as question answering, text summarization, decision support etc. While encyclopaedic knowledge can be manually encoded into causal relations, in many other domains, causality is not explicit and must be inferred from data. The EACL Workshop on Computational Approaches to Causality in Language provides a forum for presentation and discussion of innovative research on all aspects of recognition, representation and the use of causal information and its processing in NLP-centered applications.

These proceedings contain papers presented at the workshop held in Gothenburg, Sweden on April 26 2014, in conjunction with the 14th Conference of the European Chapter of the Association for Computational Linguistics. We received 12 papers which were reviewed by the members of the workshop program committee, and accepted 7 of them.

I would like to thank all submitting authors for their work. I also would like to thank the members of the program committee for an outstanding job in reviewing and providing advice to the authors and to the organization committee, and the MUSE project (EU FP7-296703) for sponsoring this workshop.

Oleksandr Kolomiyets

Program Committee:

Eneko Agirre, University of the Basque Country
Steven Bethard, University of Alabama at Birmingham
Gosse Bouma, University of Groningen
Paul Buitelaar, National University of Ireland
Nate Chambers, United States Naval Academy
Peter Clark, Allen Institute for AI
Walter Daelemans, University of Antwerp
Jan De Belder, KU Leuven
Matthew Gerber, University of Virginia
Roxana Girju, University of Illinois at Urbana-Champaign
Graeme Hirst, University of Toronto
Eduard Hovy, Carnegie Mellon
Alessandro Lenci, University of Pisa
Bernardo Magnini, Fondazione Bruno Kessler
Marie-Francine Moens, KU Leuven
Vincent Ng, University of Texas at Dallas
Diarmuid Ó Séaghdha, University of Cambridge
Martha Palmer, University of Colorado at Boulder
Patrick Pantel, Microsoft Research
Isaac Persing, University of Texas at Dallas
German Rigau, San Sebastin UPV/EHU
James Pustejovsky, Brandeis University
Kenji Sagae, University of Southern California
Caroline Sporleder, Saarland University
Manfred Stede, University of Potsdam
Stan Szpakowicz, University of Ottawa
Peter Turney, National Research Council of Canada
Benjamin Van Durme, Johns Hopkins University
Piek Vossen, VU University Amsterdam

Organizers:

Oleksandr Kolomiyets, KU Leuven
Marie-Francine Moens, KU Leuven
Martha Palmer, University of Colorado at Boulder
James Pustejovsky, Brandeis University
Steven Bethard, University of Alabama at Birmingham

Table of Contents

Conference Program

Saturday, April 26, 2014

9:15–9:30 Opening Remarks

Session 1

9:30–10:00 *Because We Say So*
Julie Hunter and Laurence Danlos

Automatic detection of causal relations in German multilogs
Tina Bögel, Annette Hautli-Janisz, Sebastian Sulger and Miriam Butt

10:30–11:00 Coffee Break

Studying the Semantic Context of two Dutch Causal Connectives
Iris Hendrickx and Wilbert Spooren

Annotating causality in the TempEval-3 corpus
Paramita Mirza, Rachele Sprugnoli, Sara Tonelli and Manuela Speranza

Building a Japanese Corpus of Temporal-Causal-Discourse Structures Based on SDRT for Extracting Causal Relations
Kimi Kaneko and Daisuke Bekki

Likelihood of external causation in the structure of events
Tanja Samardzic and Paola Merlo

Recognizing Causality in Verb-Noun Pairs via Noun and Verb Semantics
Mehwish Riaz and Roxana Girju

Because We Say So

Julie Hunter
Alpage
Université Paris Diderot/INRIA
juliehunter@gmail.com

Laurence Danlos
Alpage
Université Paris Diderot/INRIA
Laurence.Danlos@inria.fr

Abstract

In this paper, we show that contingency connectives, which mark causal and conditional relations (PDTB Group, 2008), restrict the possible interpretations of reports in their scope in a way that many other connectives, such as contrastive connectives, do not. We argue that this result has immediate implications for the semantics of causal relations and for the annotation of implicit connectives. In particular, it shows that the assumption, implicit in some work on NLP, that the semantics of explicit connectives can be translated to implicit connectives is not anodyne.

1 Introduction

In addition to their standard intensional use, many embedding verbs have a semantically *parenthetical use* (Urmson, 1952; Simons, 2007), in which the content of the embedded clause conveys the main point of the report. Semantically parenthetical uses can occur even when the report is not syntactically parenthetical, as shown in (1) and (2). In these examples, the embedded clause *he is out of town* (labeled 'β') conveys the main point because its content offers an explanation of Fred's absence.

(1) - [Why didn't Fred come to my party?]$_\alpha$
- Jane said [he is out of town.]$_\beta$

(2) [Fred didn't come to my party.]$_\alpha$ Jane said [he is out of town.]$_\beta$

If the matrix clause does not contribute directly to the explanation of Fred's absence in (1) and (2), it is arguable that only the content of the β-clauses contributes to the second argument of the explanatory relations that hold in these examples. In terms of *Segmented Discourse Representation Theory* (SDRT) (Asher and Lascarides, 2003), for example, the relation QUESTION-ANSWER-PAIR in (1) should be taken to hold only between α and β; the content of the matrix clause should be likewise excluded from the second argument of EXPLANATION in (2) (Hunter et al., 2006). Similarly, the *Penn Discourse Treebank* (PDTB) would relate only α and β in (2) with implicit *because* (Dinesh et al., 2005; Prasad et al., 2006).

Given this analysis of (1) and (2), however, it is puzzling why the report in (3) cannot be understood parenthetically. On the surface, (2) and (3) differ only in that the two sentences in (2) have been connected with the subordinating conjunction *because* in (3). Yet this seemingly harmless change leads to a dramatic change in interpretive possibilities.

(3) (#)[1] Fred didn't come to my party because Jane said he is out of town.

And as we'll see in §2, the contrast between (2) and (3), heretofore unnoticed in the literature, can be replicated for all contingency relations: all contingency connectives exhibit a distaste for semantically parenthetical reports.

The contrast between (2) and (3) is surprising for a further reason, namely that many relations and connectives that do not indicate causality *do* appear to accept the embedded clauses of semantically parenthetical reports as arguments.

(4) Lots of people are coming to my party. Jane said (for example) that Fred is coming with his whole family.

(5) Fred is coming to my party, although Jane told me that Bill is not.

The report in (4) is understood parenthetically; it is the content of the embedded clause, not the matrix clause, that serves as a specific example of the

[1] We use the symbol '(#)' to mark examples containing reports that cannot be interpreted parenthetically; '(#)' does not exclude the possibility of a non-parenthetical interpretation.

claim made in the first sentence. Unlike in (3), this parenthetical reading is felicitous even when *for example* is explicit. (5) shows that semantically parenthetical reports can occur in contrastive relations, as the contrast intuitively holds between Fred's coming to the party and Bill's not coming. It also shows, given that *although* is a subordinating conjunction, that a parenthetical reading of (3) is not blocked simply by the fact that *because* is a subordinating conjunction.

The contrast between (2) and (3), as well as that between (3) and (4)/(5), has direct implications for the annotation of reports and the semantics of contingency relations. In §2, we argue for the following generalization:

(C) if a contingency relation is marked by an explicit connective that has syntactic scope over the matrix clause of a report, this report cannot have a parenthetical interpretation.

With general support for (C) in place, §3 returns to the contrast, illustrated by (2) and (3), between examples of EXPLANATION with implicit and explicit connectives. We argue that this contrast raises problems for existing discourse theories and annotation practices. §4 discusses causal connectives that have a temporal sense, e.g. *after*, which appear to be counterexamples to (C). We show that this problem is only superficial.

In what follows, we will use the term *parenthetical* to talk only about semantically parenthetical uses, unless otherwise stated. We will also adopt the notation conventions of the PDTB (PDTB Group, 2008). Each discourse connective has two arguments, Arg1 and Arg2. The text whose interpretation is the basis for Arg1 appears in italics, while the text that serves as the basis for Arg2 appears in bold. If the connective is explicit, it is underlined. An example is given in (6):

(6) *Fred didn't come to the party* because **he is out of town**.

Sections 2 and 3, like the current section, will focus exclusively on data in English, though the claims made about the data in these sections hold for the French translations of the data as well. In section 4, we will discuss a point on which the data in English and French diverge in an interesting way. In all cases, the examples that we use to motivate our analysis are constructed for the sake of simplicity. Nevertheless, our claims for English are supported by data from the PDTB and *The New York Times*, as we discuss in more detail in §5.

2 Contingency relations

In the PDTB, the class of contingency relations includes causal relations (EXPLANATION and RESULT in SDRT) and their pragmatic counterparts (EXPLANATION* and RESULT*), as well as semantic and pragmatic conditional relations. To this we add relations of purpose or GOAL, marked by connectives such as *so that* and *in order to*. For simplicity, we will adopt the vocabulary of SDRT when talking about discourse relations, e.g. using EXPLANATION when the PDTB would talk of 'reason', etc.

In section 2.1, we argue that EXPLANATION and RESULT support (C). Section 2.2 introduces an apparent counterexample to this claim but then shows that this example can easily be explained within the confines of (C). In section 2.3, we show that EXPLANATION* and RESULT* pattern with their semantic counterparts with regard to parenthetical reports, and section 2.4 rounds out the discussion of contingency connectives by showing that CONDITION and GOAL support (C) as well.

2.1 Semantic explanations and results

EXPLANATION is lexically marked by the conjunctions *because*, *since*, *after*, *when*, *now that*, *as* and *for*; there are no adverbials that lexicalize this relation. *Since*, like *because*, supports (C).

(7) a. *Fred can't come to my party* since **he's out of town**.
b. (#) Fred can't come to my party since Jane said he's out of town.

The remaining causal conjunctions follow suit, but due to particularities that arise from their temporal nature, we delay our discussion of them until §4.

RESULT is lexicalized only by adverbial connectives: *therefore, hence, consequently, as a result, so, ...* and these connectives appear to pattern with markers of EXPLANATION with regard to (C). In other words, if the matrix clause falls in the syntactic scope of the adverbial, it falls in the discourse scope of the adverbial as well.

Demonstrating that (C) holds for RESULT adverbials requires care, because adverbials, unlike conjunctions, can move around. Consider (8):

(8) Fred didn't go to the party. $(H,)_1$ Jane said $(,H,)_2$ that Luc $(, H,)_3$ did $(, H)_4$.

However could be inserted in one of any of the four locations marked with 'H' above to make the example felicitous. Yet to test whether *however* allows parenthetical readings of reports in its syntactic scope, only position 2 matters. Even when *however* is in position 1, syntactic scope over the matrix clause is not ensured, as the placement of the adverbial could be the result of extraction from the embedded clause (Kroch and Joshi, 1987; Pollard and Sag, 1994).

Once we restrict our attention to adverbials in position 2, we can see more clearly that some allow parenthetical readings of reports in their syntactic scope while others do not. A parenthetical reading of the report in (8) is permitted with *however* in position 2. By contrast, the placement of *afterwards* in the matrix clause of (9) blocks a parenthetical reading.

(9) *Fred went to Dax for Christmas.* **Jane said** afterwards **that he went to Pau**.

To the extent that (9) is felicitous, the second sentence cannot be rephrased as *Jane said that he went to Pau afterwards* (although this would be a possible rephrasing of the example if *afterwards* were in position 1, 3 or 4). The more natural reading is a non-parenthetical one according to which the time at which Jane made her statement was after the time at which Fred went to Dax.

Thus we can distinguish two groups of adverbials: (i) adverbs that when they have syntactic scope over the matrix clause of a report do not allow parenthetical readings of that report, e.g. *afterwards*, and (ii) adverbs that, given the same syntactic configuration, *do* allow a parenthetical reading of the report, e.g. *however*. We can then extend these groups to discourse connectives in general, including conjunctions. In these terms, *because* falls in group (i), because it conforms to (C), and *although*, in group (ii).

With the foregoing discussion of adverbials in mind, we return now to RESULT and the question of whether RESULT adverbials fall in group (i) or group (ii). Consider (10):

(10) a. *Fred drank too much last night.* Therefore, **he has a hangover today**.

b. *Fred drank too much last night,* **Jane said/thinks**, therefore, **that he has a hangover today**.

A parenthetical reading of the report in (10b) would be one in which the content of the matrix clause does not contribute to the second argument of RESULT. In the case of (2), we said that the act of Jane's *saying* that Fred is out of town in no way explains Fred's absence—only the content of what she said matters. Yet a parallel analysis is not obviously correct for (10b) (which is why we have included the matrix clause of the report in Arg2 above). While if Jane is right, it is true that Fred's hangover is the result of his over zealous drinking, it is also reasonable to say that Jane's conclusions are the result of Fred's drinking too much: it was his drinking that prompted her to say or think what she does. We conclude that *therefore* falls in group (i) and, more generally, that RESULT supports (C).

2.2 A clarification

Before moving on to pragmatic causal relations, let's take a closer look at examples of EXPLANATION in which the source of an indirect speech report in the scope of *because* is also the agent of the eventuality described in Arg1. At first glance, such cases might appear to be counterexamples to (C), because the report in the syntactic scope of *because* does not provide a literal explanation of the eventuality described in Arg1.

(11) *Jane didn't hire Bill* because **she said he didn't give a good interview**.

It is presumably not the case that Jane did not hire Bill because she *said* he didn't interview well, but rather because she *thought* that he didn't do well.

Yet in (11), the author is not even weakly committed to the claim that Bill's interview performance is responsible for his not being hired, so the report cannot have a parenthetical interpretation (thus we have placed the matrix clause in boldface above). And if the report is non-parenthetical, then (11) is not problematic; *because* readily allows non-parenthetical readings of reports in its syntactic scope, as illustrated in (12a) and (12b).

(12) a. *Jane didn't hire Bill* because **she thought he didn't give a good interview**.

b. *Jane didn't hire Bill* because **her secretary said/thought that Bill didn't give a good interview**.

The only feature that sets (11) off from the mundane examples in (12) is the fact that Jane's act of saying what she did does not provide a literal explanation for her hiring decision. We think that the use of an indirect speech report is permitted despite this fact only because Jane is both the agent of Arg1 and the source of the report in Arg2. The assumed close tie between an agent's thoughts and actions, together with the semantics of *because*, allow us to conclude in (11) that Jane *thought* Bill didn't do well—the real explanation proffered for her hiring decision.

Interestingly, despite the non-parenthetical reading of the report in (11), this example can be reformulated with a syntactic parenthetical:

(13) *Jane didn't hire Bill* because, **she said, he didn't give a good interview**.

This is interesting because normally a syntactic parenthetical construction would be taken to entail a semantically parenthetical construction. Yet we do not think that the speaker is required to accept the content of Jane's report in (13) any more than she is in (11). The use of the syntactic parenthetical appears rather to distance the speaker's point of view from Jane's. But as we argued for the phenomenon illustrated in (11), we think that the non-parenthetical interpretation of the syntactically parenthetical report in (13) is made possible only by the fact that the agent of Arg1 is the source of the report in Arg2 of EXPLANATION.

2.3 Pragmatic explanations and results

Pragmatic result, or RESULT* in SDRT, holds between two clauses α and β when α provides justification for the author's affirmation of β. In other words, RESULT*(Arg1, Arg2) if and only if RESULT(Arg1, affirm(author, Arg2)). In examples (14a-c), Arg1 does not provide an explanation of the conclusion drawn in Arg2 (the accumulation of newspapers did not cause the neighbors to be out of town), but rather of why the speaker or Jane formed the belief that the conclusion holds. (14b) and (14c) are examples of RESULT because they make this causal relation explicit with *I think* or *Jane said/thinks*. (14a), an example of RESULT*, leaves this connection implicit. (In order to visually signal the presence of a pragmatic relation in the examples in this section, we mark the corresponding connectives with a '*'.)

(14) a. *The newspapers are piling up on the neighbors' stoop.* Therefore*, **they must be out of town.**

b. *The newspapers are piling up on the neighbors' stoop.* **I think**, therefore, **that they must be out of town.**

c. *The newspapers are piling up on the neighbors' stoop.* **Jane said/thinks**, therefore, **that they must be out of town.**

Reports in examples like (14b) and (14c) cannot be read parenthetically, and the nature of RESULT* prevents its second argument from ever being a clause embedded by a parenthetically used verb.

EXPLANATION* reverses the order of explanation from RESULT*, i.e. EXPLANATION*(Arg1, Arg2) = EXPLANATION(affirm(author, Arg1), Arg2). EXPLANATION* is marked by connectives such as *since*, *because*, and *for*, which need not be explicit, hence the parentheses in (15). (15a) and (15c) are examples of EXPLANATION*, while (15b) and (15d), which explicitly evoke the speaker's belief state for Arg1, are examples of EXPLANATION.[2]

(15) a. *The neighbors must be out of town* (because*) **newspapers are piling up on their stoop**.

b. *I think that the neighbors must be out of town* because **newspapers are piling up on their stoop**.

c. *The neighbors must be out of town* (because*) **Jane said that newspapers are piling up on their stoop.**

d. *I think that the neighbors must be out of town* because **Jane said that newspapers are piling up on their stoop**.

In both (15c) and (15d), the matrix clause *Jane said* contributes to Arg2, i.e. the reports are not parenthetical. These examples are not like (2) because the fact that the evidence comes from Jane is crucial in the formation of the speaker's belief that the neighbors are out of town in (15c,d) in a way that it is not crucial to Fred's absence in (2). In all three examples, there is a reasoning process involved in which Jane figures, but the reasoning process is not the main point of (2) in the way that it is for (15c) and (15d).

In §3 we will provide a further reason why (15c) should not be considered parenthetical. This argument, together with those given in this section, in turn supports our claim that connectives that mark causal relations are members of group (i) of discourse connectives, regardless of whether they

[2]We assume that for Jane to sincerely say that P, Jane must believe P; it might be more accurate to talk about Jane's commitments rather than her beliefs, but that detail is not important here.

mark semantic or pragmatic relations. That is, these connectives conform to (C).

2.4 Other contingency relations

A quick review of the remaining contingency relations shows that principle (C) is obeyed throughout this class. GOAL can be lexically marked by the subordinating conjunctions *in order that* and *so that*; semantic conditional relations are generally marked by the conjunction *if*. In all cases, principle (C) is respected because the reports in examples like (16b) and (17b) cannot be understood parenthetically.

(16) a. *Fred made a pizza last night* so that **Mary would be happy**.
b. * Fred made a pizza last night so that Jane said/thinks that Mary would be happy.

(17) a. *Fred will play tennis* if **Mary doesn't show up**.
b. (#) Fred will play tennis if Jane said/thinks that Mary won't show up.

3 Commitment and veridicality

Now that we have shown that contingency relations support (C), we return to the contrast between (2) and (3) and discuss the problems that this contrast raises for existing theories of discourse and annotation.

In (15c) note that while the verb *say* could be replaced by, for example, *noticed* or *told me*, it cannot be replaced by *believe* or *thinks*.

(18) # The neighbors must be out of town because Jane thinks that newspapers are piling up on their stoop.

(18) can be repaired, however, by weakening the modal in Arg1 from *must* to *might*:

(19) *The neighbors might be out of town* (because) **Jane thinks that newspapers are piling up on their stoop.**

This follows from the semantics of EXPLANATION*, which holds when Arg2 is presented as *the* reason for drawing the conclusion given in Arg1. The speaker is not entitled to draw a stronger conclusion than her evidence allows. The use of *thinks* in (18) implies that Jane is not fully committed to the claim that newspapers are piling up on the neighbor's doorstep, so the speaker is only entitled to affirm a possibility claim like that in Arg1 of (19). Thus (18) is infelicitous for the same reason that (20) is not an example of EXPLANATION*: Jane's saying what she did does not justify the conclusion that the neighbors are out of town (Danlos and Rambow, 2011).

(20) The neighbors must be out of town. Jane said that newspapers are piling up on their stoop, but that's not why I think they're gone.

In contrast to (18), (2) is felicitous with *thinks*:

(21) *Fred didn't come to my party*. Jane thinks **he's out of town**.

In (21), the author's commitment to Fred's absence is allowed to be higher than Jane's commitment to his being out of town. This is because Jane's saying what she did is not presented as the justification of the author's belief that Fred wasn't at the party. The author has other reasons for thinking and saying that Fred was not at his party; now he's exploring reasons for Fred's absence. Thus the contrast between (18) and (21) provides further support for our claim in §2.3 that the report in (15c) is not parenthetical; the semantics of the report in (15c) affect the acceptability of the example.

The foregoing discussion of parenthetical reports has implications for the *veridicality* of discourse relations. In SDRT, which provides a theory not only of discourse structure but also of the interpretation of that structure, EXPLANATION and RESULT, along with their pragmatic counterparts, are *veridical* relations, where a relation R is veridical just in case if $R(\alpha, \beta)$ is true at a world w, then α and β are true at w as well. In the case of causal relations, for it to be true that one eventuality caused another, it must be the case that both eventualities truly occurred. In this paper, we have limited our study of parenthetical reports to the right argument (Arg2) of discourse relations. Accordingly, we will limit our discussion of veridicality to *right*-veridicality.

From the data that we have so far, it is clear that EXPLANATION* is right veridical: if Arg2 isn't true, it cannot justify Arg1. Even in the case of (15c), while what Jane said can be false, it must be true that Jane said what she said. Likewise, the data that we have discussed for RESULT, RESULT*, GOAL and conditional relations indicate that these relations are also right-veridical.

The question is more complicated for EXPLANATION. A speaker who asserts (2) or (21) and offers Jane's comment as an explanation is not fully committed to Fred's being out of town. This is clear in (21), where the verb *think* indicates a hedged commitment. Thus, if we analyze the reports in (2) and (21) as parentheticals, then right veridicality is not ensured for EXPLANATION, at least when unmarked by an explicit connective.

When EXPLANATION is explicitly marked with *because*, *since*, or *for*, right veridicality appears to be ensured by the fact that these conjunctions block parenthetical readings of reports in their syntactic scope. Yet (3), repeated as (22a), is greatly improved if we use a syntactic parenthetical, which suggests that its infelicity has more to do with syntax than with veridicality:

(22) a. (#) Fred didn't come to my party because Jane said he is out of town.
b. *Fred didn't come to my party* because, Jane said, **he is out of town**.

However, note that *said* in (22b) cannot be replaced with a weaker embedding verb like *thinks*:

(23) # Fred didn't come to my party because, Jane thinks, he is out of town.

This shows that even though a syntactic parenthetical is used in (22b), the speaker must be fully committed to the content of Arg2, i.e. right veridicality is ensured for EXPLANATION when it is explicitly marked with *because*.

We have seen that EXPLANATION is right veridical when explicitly marked, but that (2) does not require the veridicality of the clause labeled 'β'. This difference forces us to make a choice. We can maintain the claim that (2) is nevertheless an example of EXPLANATION; in this case, we must adjust the semantics of EXPLANATION accordingly and conclude that veridicality is a requirement imposed by connectives, not relations. Alternatively, we can maintain that EXPLANATION is always (right) veridical; in this case, we must give up the claim that (2) is an example of EXPLANATION.

We suspect that the second choice is better. There is, after all, no connective that can be inserted between the sentences in (2) in such a way that the meaning is preserved, which suggests that a deep semantic difference is at play between (2) and examples of EXPLANATION. Either way, however, existing theories of discourse structure will need to be adjusted to account for our observations on contingency relations and parenthetical reports. For example, if (2) is not a genuine example of EXPLANATION, SDRT needs to offer a viable alternative relation. On the other hand, if (2) is a genuine example of EXPLANATION, SDRT needs to adjust the notion of veridicality in the semantics of this relation and indeed, of any other supposedly veridical discourse relations that allow their Arg2 to be the embedded clause of a parenthetical report.

Our observations also raise questions about the semantic implications of the choice made in the PDTB to insert an implicit connective in the absence of an explicit one. While this choice was a practical one meant to facilitate the annotation task for the PDTB, it has been taken to further levels in other work on NLP, and we think this is dangerous from a semantic point of view. While NLP systems designed to identify discourse relations in the presence of explicit connectors have yielded very positive results (f-scores over 90% for guessing one of the four major PDTB sense classes, i.e. Temporal, Contingency, Comparison and Expansion (Pitler and Nenkova, 2009)), the task of identifying discourse relations that hold between spans of text has proven very difficult in the absence of explicit connectives. To handle the latter type of case, systems have been designed that use the deletion of explicit connectives, whose semantics are known, to obtain examples with implicit connectives that inherit the semantics of their explicit counterparts in an effort to create new data that can be exploited in the identification of implicit relations (Marcu and Echihabi, 2002). In the other direction, systems have been built to predict implicit discourse connectives between two textual units with the use of a language model (Zhou et al., 2010).

In both kinds of systems, deleting an explicit connective or adding an implicit connective is considered a harmless move, though this practice has been questioned by (Sporleder and Lascarides, 2008). The data presented in this paper show that the presence or absence of a discourse connective may drastically change the data when reports of saying or attitudes occur in the second argument of a discourse relation — positing an implicit *because* in (2) is not an anodyne move from a semantic point of view.

4 Temporal relations

While *afterwards* falls in group (i) of discourse connectives, because it does not allow parenthetical readings of reports in its scope, as shown in (9), other temporal markers appear to fall in group (ii). Consider, for example, *after* and *before* in (24a) and (24b), respectively.

(24) a. *Fred arrived at the scene*$_\alpha$ after [police say]$_\beta$ [the crime occurred.]$_\gamma$
b. *Fred had tried to improve his life*$_\alpha$ before [police say]$_\beta$ [he robbed a bank.]$_\gamma$

Both (24a) and (24b) have a reading according to which the temporal relation indicated by the underlined conjunction holds between the clauses α and γ rather than α and β, which suggests that the reports are parenthetical. The fact that the relation between α and β can be independent of the temporal constraints of the connective is clearest in (24a) in which the time of β can actually be after the time of α.

The possibility that temporal connectives allow parenthetical readings of reports in their scope is potentially problematic for our arguments in §2 because some temporal connectives, such as *after*, *now that*, *as* and *when*, can have a causal sense in addition to their temporal sense. And when they do, parenthetical reports still appear to be possible, as shown in (25):

(25) *Fred was arrested*$_\alpha$ after [police say]$_\beta$ [he pulled a gun on an officer.]$_\gamma$

In (25), we understand the arrest as a result of Fred's pulling a gun on an officer, so *after* has a causal sense. Nevertheless, the time of β can come after the time of α, thus suggesting a parenthetical report.

Interestingly, the data on *after* and *before* in English are not supported cross-linguistically. Up to example (24), all of the data that we have discussed are felicitous in French if and only if they are felicitous in English,[3] but this is not so for (24) and (25), whose French counterparts are syntactically ill-formed.

(26) a. * Fred est arrivé sur les lieux après que la police dit/dise que le crime a eu lieu.
b. * Fred a essayé d'améliorer sa vie avant que la police dise qu'il a cambriolé une banque.
c. * Fred a été arrêté après que la police dit/dise qu'il a pointé un pistolet sur un policier.

The parenthetical reading of the report in (25) is greatly aided by the use of the present tense on *say*, which excludes the possibility that the matrix clause introduces an eventuality that held before Fred was arrested. For whatever reason, the use of the present and/or present subjunctive in similar environments is not allowed in French, as shown in (26). This difference could be taken two ways. Perhaps *after* does violate (C) after all and the only reason that parenthetical readings are blocked in (26) is because French syntax does not allow this reading to be brought out. On the other hand, it could be that *after* does support (C), but that *police say* in (25) is not functioning as a standard matrix clause.

Evidence for the second option, which is consistent with (C), comes from the fact that all of the examples that we have found like (25) come from newspapers and involve a matrix clause like *police say* (*parents say*, *teachers say*, ...) and can be paraphrased using *allegedly* instead of *police say*:

(27) *Fred was arrested* after **he allegedly pulled a gun on an officer**.

Parenthetical readings do not appear to be possible for reports in which the matrix clause cannot be paraphrased with *allegedly*, as shown in (28):

(28) (?) Fred revised his negative opinion of Paris after Jane says/said he had a wonderful visit there last summer.

If the result in (25) does not generalize to standard reports like that in (28), it is unlikely that the interpretation of the report in (25) should be explained in terms of the causal nature of *after*; it is far more likely to be due to an idiosyncracy of the matrix clause *police say*.

In any case, a full discussion of examples like (25) is not directly relevant to the discussion of causality in this paper. For the temporal connectives that can have a causal sense (*after*, *now that*, *when*, *as*, and their French counterparts), it is the case in both French and English that when they have a causal + temporal sense, their interpretative possibilities match those in which these connectives have a purely temporal sense. This fact, combined with the fact that these connectives rarely if ever have a purely causal sense, tells us that their

[3]Some of the data presented in this paper are discussed for French in (Danlos, 2013).

temporal nature is more fundamental. So (25) is not a direct challenge to the arguments that we have made in this paper about causal relations and parenthetical reports.

Let's return to (C):

(C) if a contingency relation is marked by an explicit connective that has syntactic scope over the matrix clause of a report, this report cannot have a parenthetical interpretation.

We conclude that this generalization holds for all contingency relations and markers with a purely causal or otherwise contingent sense. We furthermore predict that if there are examples in which either *after*, *now that*, *when* or *as* has a purely causal interpretation, in none of these examples will we find a parenthetical reading of a report in the connective's syntactic scope.

5 Conclusion

In this paper, we have examined the interaction between contingency connectives and the interpretation of reports that fall in their syntactic scope. We have shown that contrary to certain other types of connectives, such as contrastive connectives like *although* and *however*, contingency connectives restrict the interpretations of reports in their scope so that these reports must be interpreted non-parenthetically. That is, contingency connectives support (C). We argued that this result has immediate implications for theories of discourse structure and annotation. In particular, SDRT must either adjust the semantics of EXPLANATION to include examples like (2), which are not right-veridical, or introduce a new relation to handle (2). And the assumption that one can move between implicit and explicit connectors—an assumption made for practical reasons in the PDTB but taken to further extremes in other work on NLP described in §3—is not semantically innocent.

Throughout this paper, we have used constructed examples to simplify the discussion. However, data from the PDTB provide support for our claims in the sense that it provides no counterexamples to (C) with *because* or *since*. We found only 6 results for a search of the PDTB with the following criteria: explicit relation + (connector = *because*) + (Arg2 Source = Other). Our aim was to find examples in which a report is in the syntactic scope of *because*. Of the 6 examples that we found, two involved continuations of direct quotations and so did not have an explicit matrix clause, while the 4 remaining examples were of the sort discussed in §2.2, where the agent of Arg1 is the source of the report in Arg2. Nor did we find any counterexamples with an equivalent search for *since* (0 results for an equivalent search with explicit *since*).

A separate search of the PDTB revealed no violations of (C) for examples in which *now that*, *as*, and *when* have purely causal interpretations. That is, for all examples in the PDTB in which *now that*, *as*, and *when* are explicit and have a causal sense, and in which 'Arg2 Source = Other' holds, these connectors have a temporal sense as well. (There are no examples in the PDTB in which *after* has a purely causal sense). While a thorough study of temporal connectives is needed to fully understand the behavior of these conjunctions, as explained in §4, these data provide strong prima facie support for the claims made in §4.

In future work we would like to extend our study of contingency connectives, starting with temporal connectives, to see how far (C) can be generalized to other kinds of relations. We also hope to back up our results for English and French with more cross-linguistic research. In the meantime, data on contingency connectives in French and English offer clear support for (C).

References

Nicholas Asher and Alex Lascarides. 2003. *Logics of Conversation*. Cambridge University Press, Cambridge.

Laurence Danlos and Owen Rambow. 2011. Discourse Relations and Propositional Attitudes. In *Proceedings of the Constraints in Discourse Workshop (CID 2011)*, Agay, France.

Laurence Danlos. 2013. Connecteurs de discours adverbiaux: Problèmes à l'interface syntaxe-sémantique. *Linguisticae Investigationes*, 36(2):261–275.

Nikhil Dinesh, Alan Lee, Eleni Miltsakaki, Rashmi Prasad, and Aravind Joshi. 2005. Attribution and the (non-)alignment of syntactic and discourse arguments of connectives. In *Proceedings of ACL Workshop on Frontiers in Corpus Annotation*, Ann Arbor, MI, USA.

Julie Hunter, Nicholas Asher, Brian Reese, and Pascal Denis. 2006. Evidentiality and intensionality: Two uses of reportative constructions in discourse. In *Proceedings of the Constraints in Discourse Workshop (CID 2006)*, Maynoth, Ireland.

Anthony Kroch and Aravind Joshi. 1987. Analyzing extraposition in a tree adjoining grammar. *Syntax and Semantics*, 20:107–149.

Daniel Marcu and Abdessamad Echihabi. 2002. An unsupervised approach to recognizing discourse relations. *Proceedings of the ACL 2002 Conference*, pages 368–375.

PDTB Group. 2008. The Penn Discourse Treebank 2.0 annotation manual. Technical report, Institute for Research in Cognitive Science, University of Philadelphia.

Emily Pitler and Ani Nenkova. 2009. Using syntax to disambiguate explicit discourse connectives in text. *Proceedings of the ACL-IJCNLP 2009 Conference Short Papers*.

Carl Pollard and Ivan Sag. 1994. *Head-Driven Phrase Structure Grammar*. CSLI Publications, Stanford.

Rashmi Prasad, Nikhil Dinesh, Alan Lee, Aravind Joshi, and Bonnie Webber. 2006. Attribution and its annotation in the Penn Discourse Treebank. *Revue TAL*, 47(2).

Mandy Simons. 2007. Observations on embedding verbs, evidentiality, and presupposition. *Lingua*, 117(6):1034–1056.

Caroline Sporleder and Alex Lascarides. 2008. Using automatically labelled examples to classify rhetorical relations: A critical assessment. *Natural Language Engineering*, 14(3):369–416.

James Opie Urmson. 1952. Parenthetical verbs. *Lind*, 61 (244):480–496.

Zhi-Min Zhou, Yu Xu, Zheng-Yu Niu, Man Lan, Jian Su, and Chew Lim Tan. 2010. Predicting discourse connectives for implicit discourse relation recognition. In *Proceedings of the 23rd International Conference on Computational Linguistics: Posters*, COLING 2010, pages 1507–1514.

Annotating causality in the TempEval-3 corpus

Paramita Mirza
FBK, Trento, Italy
University of Trento
paramita@fbk.eu

Rachele Sprugnoli
FBK, Trento, Italy
University of Trento
sprugnoli@fbk.eu

Sara Tonelli
FBK, Trento, Italy
satonelli@fbk.eu

Manuela Speranza
FBK, Trento, Italy
manspera@fbk.eu

Abstract

While there is a wide consensus in the NLP community over the modeling of temporal relations between events, mainly based on Allen's temporal logic, the question on how to annotate other types of event relations, in particular causal ones, is still open. In this work, we present some annotation guidelines to capture causality between event pairs, partly inspired by TimeML. We then implement a rule-based algorithm to automatically identify explicit causal relations in the TempEval-3 corpus. Based on this annotation, we report some statistics on the behavior of causal cues in text and perform a preliminary investigation on the interaction between causal and temporal relations.

1 Introduction

The annotation of events and event relations in natural language texts has gained in recent years increasing attention, especially thanks to the development of TimeML annotation scheme (Pustejovsky et al., 2003), the release of TimeBank (Pustejovsky et al., 2006) and the organization of several evaluation campaigns devoted to automatic temporal processing (Verhagen et al., 2007; Verhagen et al., 2010; UzZaman et al., 2013).

However, while there is a wide consensus in the NLP community over the modeling of temporal relations between events, mainly based on Allen's interval algebra (Allen, 1983), the question on how to model other types of event relations is still open. In particular, linguistic annotation of causal relations, which have been widely investigated from a philosophical and logical point of view, are still under debate. This leads, in turn, to the lack of a standard benchmark to evaluate causal relation extraction systems, making it difficult to compare systems performances, and to identify the state-of-the-art approach for this particular task.

Although several resources exist in which causality has been annotated, they cover only few aspects of causality and do not model it in a global way, comparable to what as been proposed for temporal relations in TimeML. See for instance the annotation of causal arguments in PropBank (Bonial et al., 2010) and of causal discourse relations in the Penn Discourse Treebank (The PDTB Research Group, 2008).

In this work, we propose annotation guidelines for causality inspired by TimeML, trying to take advantage of the clear definition of events, signals and relations proposed by Pustejovsky et al. (2003). Besides, as a preliminary investigation of causality in the TempEval-3 corpus, we perform an automatic analysis of causal signals and relations observed in the corpus. This work is a first step towards the annotation of the TempEval-3 corpus with causality, with the final goal of investigating the strict connection between temporal and causal relations. In fact, there is a temporal constraint in causality, i.e. the cause must occur BEFORE the effect. We believe that investigating this precondition on a corpus basis can contribute to improving the performance of temporal and causal relation extraction systems.

2 Existing resources on Causality

Several attempts have been made to annotate causal relations in texts. A common approach is to look for specific cue phrases like *because* or *since* or to look for verbs that contain a cause as part of their meaning, such as *break* (*cause to be broken*) or *kill* (*cause to die*) (Khoo et al., 2000; Sakaji et al., 2008; Girju et al., 2007). In PropBank (Bonial et al., 2010), causal relations are annotated in the form of predicate-argument relations, where ARGM-CAU is used to annotate "the reason for an action", for example: *"They* [PREDICATE ***moved***] *to London* [ARGM-CAU ***because of the baby***]*."*

Another scheme annotates causal relations between discourse arguments, in the framework of the Penn Discourse Treebank (PDTB). As opposed to PropBank, this kind of relations holds only between clauses and do not involve predicates and their arguments. In PDTB, the *Cause* relation type is classified as a subtype of CONTINGENCY.

Causal relations have also been annotated as relations between events in a restricted set of linguistic constructions (Bethard et al., 2008), between clauses in text from novels (Grivaz, 2010), or in noun-noun compounds (Girju et al., 2007).

Several types of annotation guidelines for causal relations have been presented, with varying degrees of reliability. One of the simpler approaches asks annotators to check whether the sentence they are reading can be paraphrased using a connective phrase such as *and as a result* or *and as a consequence* (Bethard et al., 2008).

Another approach to annotate causal relations tries to combine linguistic tests with semantic reasoning tests. In Grivaz (2010), the linguistic paraphrasing suggested by Bethard et al. (2008) is augmented with rules that take into account other semantic constraints, for instance if the potential cause occurs before or after the potential effect.

3 Annotation of causal information

As part of a wider annotation effort aimed to annotate texts at the semantic level (Tonelli et al., 2014), we propose guidelines for the annotation of causal information. In particular, we define causal relations between events based on the TimeML definition of events (ISO TimeML Working Group, 2008), as including all types of actions (punctual and durative) and states. Syntactically, events can be realized by a wide range of linguistic expressions such as verbs, nouns (which can realize eventualities in different ways, for example through a nominalization process of a verb or by possessing an eventive meaning), and prepositional constructions.

Following TimeML, our annotation of events involved in causal relations includes the `polarity` attribute (see Section 3.3); in addition to this, we have defined the `factuality` and `certainty` event attributes, which are useful to infer information about actual causality between events.

Parallel to the TimeML tag <SIGNAL> as an indicator for temporal links, we have also introduced the notion of causal signals through the use of the <C-SIGNAL> tag.

3.1 C-SIGNAL

The <C-SIGNAL> tag is used to mark-up textual elements that indicate the presence of a causal relation (i.e. a CLINK, see 3.2). Such elements include all causal uses of:

- prepositions, e.g. *because of, on account of, as a result of, in response to, due to, from, by*;
- conjunctions, e.g. *because, since, so that, hence, thereby*;
- adverbial connectors, e.g. *as a result, so, therefore, thus*;
- clause-integrated expressions, e.g. *the result is, the reason why, that's why.*

The extent of C-SIGNALs corresponds to the whole expression, so multi-token extensions are allowed.

3.2 CLINK (Causal Relations)

For the annotation of causal relations between events, we use the <CLINK> tag, a directional one-to-one relation where the causing event is the *source* (the first argument, indicated as $_S$ in the examples) and the caused event is the *target* (the second argument, indicated as $_T$). The annotation of CLINKs includes the `c-signalID` attribute, whose value is the ID of the C-SIGNAL indicating the causal relation (if available).

A seminal research in cognitive psychology based on the force dynamics theory (Talmy, 1988) has shown that causation covers three main kinds of causal concepts (Wolff, 2007), which are CAUSE, ENABLE, and PREVENT, and that these causal concepts are lexicalized as verbs (Wolff and Song, 2003): (i) CAUSE-type verbs: *bribe, cause, compel, convince, drive, have, impel, incite, induce, influence, inspire, lead, move, persuade, prompt, push, force, get, make, rouse, send, set, spur, start, stimulate*; (ii) ENABLE-type verbs: *aid, allow, enable, help, leave, let, permit*; (iii) PREVENT-type verbs: *bar, block, constrain, deter, discourage, dissuade, hamper, hinder, hold, impede, keep, prevent, protect, restrain, restrict, save, stop*. CAUSE, ENABLE, and PREVENT categories of causation and the corresponding verbs are taken into account in our guidelines.

As causal relations are often not overtly expressed in text (Wolff et al., 2005), we restrict the annotation of CLINKs to the presence of an explicit causal construction linking two events in the same sentence[1], as detailed below:

- **Basic constructions** for CAUSE, ENABLE and PREVENT categories of causation as shown in the following examples:
  *The purchase$_S$ **caused** the creation$_T$ of the current building*
  *The purchase$_S$ **enabled** the diversification$_T$ of their business*
  *The purchase$_S$ **prevented** a future transfer$_T$*

- Expressions containing **affect verbs**, such as *affect*, *influence*, *determine*, and *change*. They can be usually rephrased using *cause*, *enable*, or *prevent*:
  *Ogun ACN crisis$_S$ **affects** the launch$_T$ of the All Progressives Congress → Ogun ACN crisis **causes/enables/prevents** the launch of the All Progressives Congress*

- Expressions containing **link verbs**, such as *link*, *lead*, and *depend on*. They can usually be replaced only with *cause* and *enable*:
  *An earthquake$_T$ in North America was **linked** to a tsunami$_S$ in Japan → An earthquake in North America was **caused/enabled** by a tsunami in Japan*
  An earthquake in North America was **prevented by a tsunami in Japan*

- **Periphrastic causatives** are generally composed of a verb that takes an embedded clause or predicate as a complement; for example, in the sentence *The blast$_S$ caused the boat to heel$_T$ violently*, the verb (i.e. *caused*) expresses the notion of CAUSE while the embedded verb (i.e. *heel*) expresses a particular result. Note that the notion of CAUSE can be expressed by verbs belonging to the three categories previously mentioned (which are CAUSE-type verbs, ENABLE-type verbs and PREVENT-type verbs).

- Expressions containing **causative conjunctions and prepositions** as listed in Section 3.1. Causative conjunctions and prepositions are annotated as C-SIGNALs and their ID is to be reported in the `c-signalID` attribute of the CLINK.[2]

In some contexts, the coordinating conjunction *and* can imply causation; given the ambiguity of this construction and the fact that it is not an explicit causal construction, however, we do not annotate CLINKs between two events connected by *and*. Similarly, the temporal conjunctions *after* and *when* can also implicitly assert a causal relation but should not be annotated as C-SIGNALs and no CLINKs are to be created (temporal relations have to be created instead).

3.3 Polarity, factuality and certainty

The `polarity` attribute, present both in TimeML and in our guidelines, captures the grammatical category that distinguishes affirmative and negative events. Its values are NEG for events which are negated (for instance, the event *cause* in *Serotonin deficiency$_S$ may **not cause** depression$_T$*) and POS otherwise.

The annotation of `factuality` that we added to our guidelines is based on the situation to which an event refers. FACTUAL is used for *facts*, i.e. situations that have happened, COUNTERFACTUAL is used for *counterfacts*, i.e. situations that have no real counterpart as they did not take place, NON-FACTUAL is used for *possibilities*, i.e. speculative situations, such as future events, events for which it is not possible to determine whether they have happened, and general statements.

The `certainty` attribute expresses the binary distinction between certain (value CERTAIN) and uncertain (value UNCERTAIN) events. Uncertain events are typically marked in the text by the presence of modals or modal adverbs (e.g. *perhaps*, *maybe*) indicating possibility. In the sentence *Drinking$_S$ may **cause** memory loss$_T$*, the causal connector *cause* is an example of a NON-FACTUAL and UNCERTAIN event.

In the annotation algorithm presented in the following section, only the `polarity` attribute is taken into account, given that information about factuality and certainty of events is not annotated in the TempEval-3 corpus. In particular, at the time of the writing the algorithm considers only the polarity of causal verbal connectors, because this information is necessary to extract causal chains

[1] A typical example of implicit causal construction is represented by lexical causatives; for example, *kill* has the embedded meaning of causing someone to die (Huang, 2012). In the present guidelines, these cases are not included.

[2] The absence of a value for the `c-signalID` attribute means that the causal relation is encoded by a verb.

between events in a text. However, adding information on the polarity of the single events involved in the relations would make possible also the identification of positive and negative causes and effects.

4 Automatic annotation of explicit causality between events

In order to verify the soundness of our annotation framework for event causality, we implement some simple rules based on the categories and linguistic cues listed in Section 3. Our goal is two-fold: first, we want to check how accurate rule-based identification of (explicit) event causality can be. Second, we want to have an estimate of how frequently causality can be explicitly found in text.

The dataset we annotate has been released for the TempEval-3 shared task[3] on temporal and event processing. The TBAQ-cleaned corpus is the training set provided for the task, consisting of the TimeBank (Pustejovsky et al., 2006) and the AQUAINT corpora. It contains around 100K words in total, with 11K words annotated as events (UzZaman et al., 2013). We choose this corpus because gold events are already provided, and because it allows us to perform further analyses on the interaction between temporal and causal relations.

Our automatic annotation pipeline takes as input the TBAQ-cleaned corpus with gold annotated events and tries to automatically recognize whether there is a causal relation holding between them. The annotation algorithm performs the following steps in sequence:

1. The TBAQ-cleaned corpus is PoS-tagged and parsed using the Stanford dependency parser (de Marneffe and Manning, 2008).

2. The corpus is further analyzed with the *addDiscourse* tagger (Pitler and Nenkova, 2009), which automatically identifies explicit discourse connectives and their sense, i.e. EXPANSION, CONTINGENCY, COMPARISON and TEMPORAL. This is used to disambiguate causal connectives (e.g. we consider only the occurrences of *since* when it is a causal connective, meaning that it falls into CONTINGENCY class instead of TEMPORAL).

3. Given the list of *affect*, *link*, *causative* verbs (basic and periphrastic constructions) and *causal signals* listed in Sections 3.1 and 3.2, the algorithm looks for specific dependency constructions where the causal verb or signal is connected to two events, as annotated in the TBAQ-cleaned corpus.

4. If such dependencies are found, a CLINK is automatically set between the two events identifying the source ($_S$) and the target ($_T$) of the relation.

5. When a causal connector corresponds to an event, the algorithm uses the polarity of the event to assign a polarity to the causal link.

Specific approaches to detect when ambiguous connectors have a causal meaning are implemented, as in the case of *from* and *by*, where the algorithm looks for specific structures. For instance, in *"The building was damaged$_T$ **by** the earthquake$_S$"*, *by* is governed by a passive verb annotated as event.

Also the preposition *due to* is ambiguous as shown in the following sentences where it acts as a causal connector only in b):

a) *It had been **due to** expire Friday evening.*

b) *It cut$_T$ the dividend **due to** its third-quarter loss$_S$ of $992,000.*

The algorithm performs the disambiguation by checking the dependency structures: in sentence a) there is only one dependency relation *xcomp(due, expire)*, while in sentence b) the dependency relations are *xcomp(cut, due)* and *prep_to(due, loss)*. Besides, both *cut* and *loss* are annotated as events.

We are aware that this type of automatic annotation may be prone to errors because it takes into account only a limited list of causal connectors. Besides, it only partially accounts for possible ambiguities of causal cues and may suffer from parsing errors. However, this allows us to make some preliminary remarks on the amount of causal information found in the TempEval-3 corpus. Some statistics are reported in the following subsection.

4.1 Statistics of Automatic Annotation

Basic construction. In Table 1 we report some statistics on the non-periphrastic structures identified starting from verbs expressing the three categories of causation. Note that for the verbs *have*, *start*, *hold* and *keep*, even though they connect two events, we cannot say that there is always a causal relation between them, as exemplified in the following sentence taken from the corpus:

a) *Gen. Schwarzkopf secretly picked$_S$ Saturday*

[3]http://www.cs.york.ac.uk/semeval-2013/task1/

night as the optimal time to ***start*** *the* *offensive*$_T$.
b) *On Tuesday, the National Abortion and Reproductive Rights Action League* *plans*$_S$ *to* ***hold*** *a news* *conference*$_T$ *to screen a TV advertisement.*

Types	Verbs	CLINK
CAUSE	have	1
	start	2
	cause	1
	compel	1
PREVENT	hold	1
	keep	3
	block	7
	prevent	1
ENABLE	-	-
Total		**17**

Table 1: Statistics of CLINKs with basic construction

Affect verbs. The algorithm does not annotate any causal relation containing affect verbs mostly because the majority of the 36 affect verb occurrences found in the corpus connect two elements that are not events, as in *"These big stocks greatly* ***influence*** *the Nasdaq Composite Index."*

Link verbs. In total, we found 50 occurrences of link verbs in the corpus, but the algorithm identifies only 4 causal links. Similar to affect verbs, this is mainly due to the fact that two events are not found to be involved in the relation. For instance, the system associated only one CLINK to *link* (out of 12 occurrences of the verb) and no CLINKs to *depend* (which occurs 3 times). Most of the CLINKs identified are signaled by the verb *lead*; for example, *"Pol Pot is considered responsible for the radical* *policies*$_S$ *that* ***led*** *to the* *deaths*$_T$ *of as many as 1.7 million Cambodians."*

Periphrastic causative verbs. Overall, there are around 1K potential occurrences of periphrastic causative verbs in the corpus. However, the algorithm identifies only around 14% of them as part of a periphrastic construction, as shown in Table 2. This is because some verbs are often used in non-periphrastic structures, e.g. *make*, *have*, *get*, *keep* and *hold*. Among the 144 cases of periphrastic constructions, 41 causal links are found by our rules.

In Table 2, for each verb type, we report the list of verbs that appear in periphrastic constructions in the corpus, specifying the number of CLINKs identified by the system for each of them.

Some other CAUSE-type (*move, push, drive, influence, compel, spur*), PREVENT-type (*hold, save, impede, deter, discourage, dissuade, restrict*) and ENABLE-type (*aid*) verbs occur in the corpus but are not involved in periphrastic structures. Some others do not appear in the corpus at all (*bribe, impel, incite, induce, inspire, rouse, stimulate, hinder, restrain*).

Types	Verbs	Periphr.	CLINK	All
CAUSE	have	34	0	239
	make	6	2	125
	get	1	0	50
	lead	2	1	38
	send	5	1	34
	set	2	0	23
	start	1	0	22
	force	2	1	15
	cause	3	2	12
	prompt	3	2	6
	persuade	2	1	3
	convince	1	1	2
PREVENT	keep	1	1	58
	stop	3	0	24
	block	2	2	21
	protect	2	1	15
	prevent	6	2	12
	hamper	1	0	2
	bar	1	0	1
	constrain	1	0	1
ENABLE	help	31	13	45
	leave	2	2	45
	allow	22	3	39
	permit	2	1	6
	enable	4	2	5
	let	4	3	5
Total		**144**	**41**	**848**

Table 2: Statistics of periphrastic causative verbs

Causal signals. Similar to periphrastic causative verbs, out of around 1.2K potential causal connectors found in the corpus, only 194 are automatically recognized as actual causal signals after disambiguation, as detailed in Table 3. Based on these identified causal signals, the algorithm derives 111 CLINKs.

Even though the *addDiscourse* tool labels 11 occurrences of the adverbial connector *so* as having a causal meaning, our algorithm does not annotate any CLINKs for such connector. In most cases, it is because it acts as an inter-sentential connector, while we limit the annotation of CLINKs only to events occurring within the same sentence.

CLINKs polarity. Table 4 shows the distribution of the positive and negative polarity of the detected CLINKs.

Only two cases of negated CLINKs are automatically identified in the corpus. One example is the following: *"Director of the U.S. Federal Bureau of*

Types	C-SIGNALs	Causal	CLINK	All
prep.	because of	32	11	32
	on account of	0	0	0
	as a result of	13	9	13
	in response to	7	1	7
	due to	*2*	*1*	*6*
	from	*2*	*2*	*500*
	by	*23*	*24*	*465*
conj.	because	58	37	58
	since	*26*	*19*	*72*
	so that	5	4	5
adverbial	as a result	3	0	3
	so	*11*	*0*	*69*
	therefore	4	0	4
	thus	6	2	6
	hence	0	0	0
	thereby	1	0	1
	consequently	1	1	1
clausal	the result is	0	0	0
	the reason why	0	0	0
	that is why	0	0	0
Total		**194**	**111**	**1242**

Table 3: Statistics of causal signals in CLINKs

Investigation (FBI) Louis Freeh said here Friday that U.S. air raid$_{T}$ *on Afghanistan and Sudan is* ***not*** *directly* ***linked*** *with the probe*$_{S}$ *into the August 7 bombings in east Africa."*

Connector types		POS	NEG
Basic	CAUSE	5	0
	PREVENT	12	0
	ENABLE	-	-
Affect verbs		-	-
Link verbs		3	1
Periphrastic	CAUSE	10	1
	PREVENT	6	0
	ENABLE	24	0
Total		**60**	**2**

Table 4: Statistics of CLINKs' polarity

CLINKs vs TLINKs. In total, the algorithm identifies 173 CLINKs in the TBAQ-cleaned corpus, while the total number of TLINKs between pairs of events is around 5.2K. For each detected CLINK between an event pair, we identify the underlying temporal relations (TLINKs) if any. We found that from the total of CLINKs extracted, around 33% of them have an underlying TLINK, as detailed in Table 5. Most of them are CLINKs signaled by causal signals.

For causative verbs, the *BEFORE* relation is the only underlying temporal relation type, with the exception of one *SIMULTANEOUS* relation.

As for C-SIGNALs, the distribution of temporal relation types is less homogeneous, as shown in Table 6. In most of the cases, the underlying temporal relation is *BEFORE*. In few cases, CLINKs signaled by the connector *because* overlap with an *AFTER* relation, as in *"But some analysts questioned*$_{T}$ *how much of an impact the retirement package will have,* ***because*** *few jobs will end*$_{S}$ *up being eliminated."*

In some cases, CLINKs signaled by the connector *since* match with a *BEGINS* relation. This shows that *since* expresses merely a temporal and not a causal link. As it has been discussed before, the connector *since* is highly ambiguous and the CLINK has been wrongly assigned because of a disambiguation mistake of the addDiscourse tool.

Connector types		CLINK	TLINK
Basic	CAUSE	5	2
	PREVENT	12	0
	ENABLE	-	-
Affect verbs		-	-
Link verbs		4	1
Periphrastic	CAUSE	11	1
	PREVENT	6	0
	ENABLE	24	0
C-SIGNALs		111	54
Total		**173**	**58**

Table 5: Statistics of CLINKs' overlapping with TLINKs

5 Evaluation

We perform two types of evaluation. The first is a qualitative one, and is carried out by manually inspecting the 173 CLINKs that have been automatically annotated. The second is a quantitative evaluation, and is performed by comparing the automatic annotated data with a gold standard corpus of 100 documents taken from TimeBank.

5.1 Qualitative Evaluation

The automatically annotated CLINKs have been manually checked in order to measure the precision of the adopted procedure. Out of 173 annotated CLINKs, 105 were correctly identified obtaining a precision of 0.61.

Details on precision calculated on the different types of categories and linguistic cues defined in Section 3.2 are provided in Table 7. Statistics show that performances vary widely depending on the category and linguistic cue taken into consideration. In particular, relations expressing causation of PREVENT type prove to be extremely difficult to be correctly detected with a rule-based approach: the algorithm precision is 0.25 for basic constructions and 0.17 for periphrastic constructions.

During the manual evaluation, two main types

C-SIGNALs	BEFORE	AFTER	IS_INCLUDED	BEGINS	others
because of	5	-	-	-	-
as a result of	2	-	-	-	-
in response to	1	-	-	-	-
due to	1	-	-	-	-
by	11	-	1	2	3
because	14	2	1	-	1
since	4	1	-	3	-
so that	1	-	-	-	-
thus	1	-	-	-	-
Total	**40**	**3**	**2**	**5**	**4**

Table 6: Statistics of CLINKs triggered by C-SIGNALs overlapping with TLINKs

Connector types		Extracted	Correct	P
Basic	CAUSE	5	3	0.60
	PREVENT	12	3	0.25
	ENABLE	0	n.a.	n.a.
Affect Verbs		0	n.a.	n.a.
Link Verbs		4	3	0.75
Periphrastic	CAUSE	11	8	0.73
	PREVENT	6	1	0.17
	ENABLE	24	17	0.71
C-SIGNALs		111	70	0.63
Total		**173**	**105**	**0.61**

Table 7: Precision of automatically annotated CLINKs

of mistakes have been observed: the wrong identification of events involved in CLINKs and the annotation of sentences that do not contain causal relations.

The assignment of a wrong source or a wrong target to a CLINK is primarily caused by the dependency parser output that tends to establish a connection between a causal verb or signal and the closest previous verb. For example, in the sentence *"StatesWest Airlines said it withdrew$_T$ its offer to acquire Mesa Airlines **because** the Farmington carrier did not respond$_S$ to its offer"*, the CLINK is annotated between *respond* and *acquire* instead of between *respond* and *withdrew*. On the other hand, dependency structure is very effective in identifying cases where one event is the consequence or the cause of multiple events, as in *"The president offered to offset$_T$ Jordan's costs **because** 40% of its exports go$_S$ to Iraq and 90% of its oil comes$_S$ from there."* In this case, the algorithm annotates a causal link between *go* and *offset*, and also between *comes* and *offset*.

The annotation of CLINKs in sentences not containing causal relations is strongly related to the ambiguous nature of many verbs, prepositions and conjunctions, which encode a causal meaning or express a causal relation only in some specific contexts. For instance, many mistakes are due to the erroneous disambiguation of the conjunction *since*. According to the addDiscourse tool, *since* is a causal connector in around one third of the cases, as in *"For now, though, that would be a theoretical advantage **since** the authorities have admitted they have no idea where Kopp is."* However, there are many cases where the outcome of the tool is not perfect, as in *"**Since** then, 427 fugitives have been taken into custody or located, 133 of them as a result of citizen assistance, the FBI said"*, where *since* acts as a temporal conjunction.

5.2 Quantitative Evaluation

In order to perform also a quantitative evaluation of our automatic annotation, we manually annotated 100 documents taken from the TimeBank corpus according to the annotation guidelines discussed before. We then used this data set as a gold standard.

The agreement reached by two annotators on a subset of 5 documents is 0.844 Dice's coefficient on C-SIGNALS (micro-average over markables) and of 0.73 on CLINKS.

We found that there are several cases where the algorithm failed to recognize causal links due to events that were originally not annotated in TimeBank. Therefore, as we proceed with the manual annotation, we also annotated missing events that are involved in causal relations. Table 8 shows that, in creating the gold standard, we annotated 61 new events. As a result, we have around 52% increase in the number of CLINKs. Nevertheless, explicit causal relations between events are by far less frequent than temporal ones, with an average of 1.4 relations per document.

If we compare the coverage of automatic annotation with the gold standard data (without newly added events, to be fair), we observe that automatic annotation covers around 76% of C-SIGNALs and only around 55% of CLINKs. This is due to the limitation of the algorithm that only considers a

Annotation	EVENT	C-SIGNAL	CLINK
manual	3933	78	144
manual-w/o new events	3872	78	95
automatic	3872	59	52

Table 8: Statistics of causality annotation in manual versus automatic annotation

	precision	recall	F1-score
C-SIGNAL	0.64	0.49	0.55
CLINK	0.42	0.23	0.30

Table 9: Automatic annotation performance

small list of causal connectors. Some examples of manually annotated causal signals that are not in the list used by the algorithm include *due mostly to*, *thanks in part to* and *in punishment for*.

Finally, we evaluate the performance of the algorithm for automatic annotation (shown in Table 9) by computing precision, recall and F1 on gold standard data without newly added events. We observe that our rule-based approach is too rigid to capture the causal information present in the data. In particular, it suffers from low recall as regards CLINKs. We believe that this issue may be alleviated by adopting a supervised approach, where the list of verbs and causal signals would be included in a larger feature set, considering among others the events' position, their PoS tags, the dependency path between the two events, etc.

6 Conclusions

In this paper, we presented our guidelines for annotating causality between events. We further tried to automatically identify in TempEval-3 corpus the types of causal relations described in the guidelines by implementing some simple rules based on causal cues and dependency structures.

In a manual revision of the annotated causal links, we observe that the algorithm obtains a precision of 0.61, with some issues related to the class of PREVENT verbs. Some mistakes are introduced by the tools used for parsing and for disambiguating causal signals, which in turn impact on our annotation algorithm. Another issue, more related to recall, is that in the TBAQ-cleaned corpus not all events are annotated, because it focuses originally on events involved in temporal relations. Therefore, the number of causal relations identified automatically would be higher if we did not take into account this constraint.

From the statistics presented in Section 4.1, we can observe that widely used verbs such as *have* or *keep* express causality relations only in few cases. The same holds for affect verbs, which are never found in the corpus with a causal meaning, and for link verbs. This shows that the main sense of causal verbs usually reported in the literature is usually the non-causal one.

Recognizing CLINKs based on causal signals is more straightforward, probably because very frequent ones such as *because of* and *as a result* are not ambiguous. Others, such as *by*, can be identified based on specific syntactic constructions.

As for the polarity of CLINKs, which is a very important feature to discriminate between actual and negated causal relations, this phenomenon is not very frequent (only 2 cases) and can be easily identified through dependency relations.

We chose to automatically annotate TBAQ-cleaned corpus because one of our goals was to investigate how TLINKs and CLINKs interact. However, this preliminary study shows that there are only few overlaps between the two relations, again with C-SIGNALs being more informative than causal verbs. This may be biased by the fact that, according to our annotation guidelines, only explicit causal relations are annotated. Introducing also the implicit cases would probably increase the overlap between TLINKs and CLINKs, because annotator would be allowed to capture the temporal constrains existing in causal relations even if the are not overtly expressed.

In the near future, we will complete the manual annotation of TempEval-3 corpus with causal information in order to have enough data for training a supervised system, in which we will incorporate the lessons learnt with this first analysis. We will also investigate the integration of the proposed guidelines into the Grounded Annotation Format (Fokkens et al., 2013), a formal framework for capturing semantic information related to events and participants at a conceptual level.

Acknowledgments

The research leading to this paper was partially supported by the European Union's 7th Framework Programme via the NewsReader Project (ICT-316404).

References

James F. Allen. 1983. Maintaining knowledge about temporal intervals. *Commun. ACM*, 26(11):832–843, November.

Steven Bethard, William Corvey, Sara Klingenstein, and James H. Martin. 2008. Building a corpus of temporal-causal structure. In European Language Resources Association (ELRA), editor, *Proceedings of the Sixth International Language Resources and Evaluation (LREC'08)*, Marrakech, Morocco, may.

Claire Bonial, Olga Babko-Malaya, Jinho D. Choi, Jena Hwang, and Martha Palmer. 2010. Propbank annotation guidelines, December. http://www.ldc.upenn.edu/Catalog/docs/LDC2011T03/propbank/english-propbank.pdf.

Marie-Catherine de Marneffe and Christopher D. Manning. 2008. The Stanford typed dependencies representation. In *Coling 2008: Proceedings of the workshop on Cross-Framework and Cross-Domain Parser Evaluation*, pages 1–8. Association for Computational Linguistics.

Antske Fokkens, Marieke van Erp, Piek Vossen, Sara Tonelli, Willem Robert van Hage, Luciano Serafini, Rachele Sprugnoli, and Jesper Hoeksema. 2013. GAF: A Grounded Annotation Framework for Events. In *Workshop on Events: Definition, Detection, Coreference, and Representation*, pages 11–20, Atlanta, Georgia, June. Association for Computational Linguistics.

Roxana Girju, Preslav Nakov, Vivi Nastase, Stan Szpakowicz, Peter Turney, and Deniz Yuret. 2007. Semeval-2007 task 04: Classification of semantic relations between nominals. In *Proceedings of the Fourth International Workshop on Semantic Evaluations (SemEval-2007)*, pages 13–18, Prague, Czech Republic, June. Association for Computational Linguistics.

Cécile Grivaz. 2010. Human Judgements on Causation in French Texts. In *Proceedings of the Seventh conference on International Language Resources and Evaluation (LREC'10)*, Valletta, Malta, may. European Language Resources Association (ELRA).

Li-szu Agnes Huang. 2012. The Effectiveness of a Corpus-based Instruction in Deepening EFL Learners' Knowledge of Periphrastic Causatives. *TESOL Journal*, 6:83–108.

ISO TimeML Working Group. 2008. ISO TC37 draft international standard DIS 24617-1, August 14. http://semantic-annotation.uvt.nl/ISO-TimeML-08-13-2008-vankiyong.pdf.

Christopher S. G. Khoo, Syin Chan, and Yun Niu. 2000. Extracting causal knowledge from a medical database using graphical patterns. In *In Proceedings of 38th Annual Meeting of the ACL, Hong Kong, 2000*, pages 336–343.

Emily Pitler and Ani Nenkova. 2009. Using syntax to disambiguate explicit discourse connectives in text. In *Proceedings of the ACL-IJCNLP 2009 Conference Short Papers*, ACLShort '09, pages 13–16, Stroudsburg, PA, USA. Association for Computational Linguistics.

James Pustejovsky, J. Castano, R. Ingria, Roser Saurí, R. Gaizauskas, A. Setzer, G. Katz, and D. Radev. 2003. TimeML: Robust specification of event and temporal expressions in text. In *Proceedings of the Fifth International Workshop on Computational Semantics*.

James Pustejovsky, Jessica Littman, Roser Saurí, and Marc Verhagen. 2006. Timebank 1.2 documentation. Technical report, Brandeis University, April.

Hiroki Sakaji, Satoshi Sekine, and Shigeru Masuyama. 2008. Extracting causal knowledge using clue phrases and syntactic patterns. In *Proceedings of the 7th International Conference on Practical Aspects of Knowledge Management*, PAKM '08, pages 111–122, Berlin, Heidelberg. Springer-Verlag.

Leonard Talmy. 1988. Force dynamics in language and cognition. *Cognitive science*, 12(1):49–100.

The PDTB Research Group. 2008. The PDTB 2.0. Annotation Manual. Technical Report IRCS-08-01, Institute for Research in Cognitive Science, University of Pennsylvania.

Sara Tonelli, Rachele Sprugnoli, and Manuela Speranza. 2014. NewsReader Guidelines for Annotation at Document Level, Extension of Deliverable D3.1. Technical Report NWR-2014-2, Fondazione Bruno Kessler. https://docs.google.com/viewer?url=http%3A%2F%2Fwww.newsreader-project.eu%2Ffiles%2F2013%2F01%2FNWR-2014-2.pdf.

Naushad UzZaman, Hector Llorens, Leon Derczynski, Marc Verhagen, James Allen, and James Pustejovsky. 2013. Semeval-2013 task 1: Tempeval-3: Evaluating events, time expressions, and temporal relations. In *Proceedings of the 7th International Workshop on Semantic Evaluation (SemEval 2013)*.

Marc Verhagen, Robert Gaizauskas, Frank Schilder, Mark Hepple, Graham Katz, and James Pustejovsky. 2007. Semeval-2007 task 15: Tempeval temporal relation identification. In *Proceedings of the Fourth International Workshop on Semantic Evaluations (SemEval-2007)*, pages 75–80, Prague, Czech Republic, June. Association for Computational Linguistics.

Marc Verhagen, Roser Saurí, Tommaso Caselli, and James Pustejovsky. 2010. Semeval-2010 task 13: Tempeval-2. In *Proceedings of the 5th International Workshop on Semantic Evaluation*, pages 57–62, Uppsala, Sweden, July. Association for Computational Linguistics.

Phillip Wolff and Grace Song. 2003. Models of causation and the semantics of causal verbs. *Cognitive Psychology*, 47(3):276–332.

Phillip Wolff, Bianca Klettke, Tatyana Ventura, and Grace Song. 2005. Expressing causation in english and other languages. *Categorization inside and outside the laboratory: Essays in honor of Douglas L. Medin*, pages 29–48.

Phillip Wolff. 2007. Representing causation. *Journal of experimental psychology: General*, 136(1):82.

Automatic detection of causal relations in German multilogs

Tina Bögel **Annette Hautli-Janisz** **Sebastian Sulger** **Miriam Butt**

Department of Linguistics
University of Konstanz
firstname.lastname@uni-konstanz.de

Abstract

This paper introduces a linguistically-motivated, rule-based annotation system for causal discourse relations in transcripts of spoken multilogs in German. The overall aim is an automatic means of determining the degree of justification provided by a speaker in the delivery of an argument in a multiparty discussion. The system comprises of two parts: A disambiguation module which differentiates causal connectors from their other senses, and a discourse relation annotation system which marks the spans of text that constitute the reason and the result/conclusion expressed by the causal relation. The system is evaluated against a gold standard of German transcribed spoken dialogue. The results show that our system performs reliably well with respect to both tasks.

1 Introduction

In general, causality refers to the way of knowing whether one state of affairs is causally related to another.[1] Within linguistics, causality has long been established as a central phenomenon for investigation. In this paper, we look at causality from the perspective of a research question from political science, where the notion is particularly important when it comes to determining (a.o.) the *deliberative* quality of a discussion. The notion of deliberation is originally due to Habermas (1981), who assumes that within a deliberative democracy, stakeholders participating in a multilog, i.e. a multi-party conversation, justify their positions truthfully, rationally and respectfully and eventually defer to the better argument. Within political science, the question arises whether actual multilogs conducted in the process of a democratic decision making indeed follow this ideal and whether/how one can use automatic means to analyze the degree of deliberativity of a multilog (Dryzek (1990; 2000), Bohman (1996), Gutmann and Thompson (1996), Holzinger and Landwehr (2010)). The disambiguation of causal discourse markers and the determination of the relations they entail is a crucial aspect of measuring the deliberative quality of a multilog. In this paper, we develop a system that is designed to perform this task.

We describe a linguistically motivated, rule-based annotation system for German which disambiguates the multiple usages of causal discourse connectors in the language and reliably annotates the reason and result/conclusion relations that the connectors introduce. The paper proceeds as follows: Section 2 briefly reviews related work on the automatic extraction and annotation of causal relations, followed by a set of examples that illustrate some of the linguistic patterns in German (Section 3). We then introduce our rule-based annotation system (Section 4) and evaluate it against a hand-crafted gold standard in Section 5, where we also present the results from the same annotation task performed by a group of human annotators. In Section 6, we provide an in-depth system error analysis. Section 7 concludes the paper.

2 Related work

The automatic detection and annotation of causality in language has been approached from various angles, for example by providing gold-standard, (manually) annotated resources such as the Penn Discourse Treebank for English (Prasad et al., 2008), which was used, e.g., in the disambiguation of English connectives by Pitler and Nenkova (2009), the Potsdam Commentary Corpus for German (Stede, 2004) and the discourse annotation layer of Tüba-D/Z, a corpus of written German text (Versley and Gastel, 2012). Training auto-

[1]This work is part of the BMBF funded eHumanities project *VisArgue*, an interdisciplinary cooperation between political science, computer science and linguistics.

matic systems that learn patterns of causality (Do et al., 2011; Mulkar-Mehta et al., 2011b, inter alia) is a crucial factor in measuring discourse coherence (Sanders, 2005), and is beneficial in approaches to question-answering (Girju, 2003; Prasad and Joshi, 2008).

With respect to automatically detecting causal relations in German, Versley (2010) uses English training data from the Penn Discourse Treebank in order to train an English annotation model. These English annotations can be projected to German in an English-German parallel corpus and on the basis of this a classifier of German discourse relations is trained. However, as previous studies have shown (Mulkar-Mehta et al., 2011a, inter alia), the reliability of detecting causal relations with automatic means differs highly between different genres. Our data consist of transcriptions of originally spoken multilogs and this type of data differs substantially from newspaper or other written texts.

Regarding the disambiguation of German connectives, Schneider and Stede (2012) carried out a corpus study of 42 German discourse connectives which are listed by Dipper and Stede (2006) as exhibiting a certain degree of ambiguity. Their results indicate that for a majority of ambiguous connectives, plain POS tagging is not reliable enough, and even contextual POS patterns are not sufficient in all cases. This is the same conclusion drawn by Dipper and Stede (2006), who also state that off-the-shelf POS taggers are too unreliable for the task. They instead suggest a mapping approach for 9 out of the 42 connectives and show that this assists considerably with disambiguation. As this also tallies with our experiments with POS taggers, we decided to implement a rule-based disambiguation module. This module takes into account contextual patterns and features of spoken communication and reliably detects causal connectors as well as the reason and result/conclusion discourse relations expressed in the connected clauses.

3 Linguistic phenomenon

In general, causality can hold between single concepts, e.g. between 'smoke' and 'fire', or between larger phrases. The phrases can be put into a causal relation via overt discourse connectors like 'because' or 'as', whereas other phrases encode causality implicitly by taking into account world knowledge about the connected events. In this paper, we restrict ourselves to the analysis of explicit discourse markers; in particular we investigate the eight most frequent German causal connectors, listed in Table 1. The *markers of reason* on the left head a subordinate clause that describes the cause of an effect stated in the matrix clause (or in the previous sentence(s)). The *markers of result/conclusion* on the other hand introduce a clause that describes the overall effect of a cause contained in the preceding clause/sentence(s). In the genre of argumentation that we are working with, the "results" tend to be logical conclusions that the speaker sees as following irrevocably from the cause presented in the argument.

Reason 'because of'	**Result** 'thus'
da	daher
weil	darum
denn	deshalb
zumal	deswegen

Table 1: German causal discourse connectors

The sentences in (1) and (2) provide examples of the phenomenon of explicit causal markers in German in our multilogs. Note that all of the causal markers in Table 1 connect a result/conclusion with a cause/reason. The difference lies in which of these relations is expressed in the clause headed by the causal connector.

The constructions in (1) and (2) exemplify this.[2] In (1), *da* 'since' introduces the reason for the conclusion in the matrix clause, i.e., the reason for the travel times being irrelevant is that they are not carried out as specified. In (2), *daher* 'thus' heads the conclusion of the reason which is provided in the matrix clause: Because the speaker has never stated a fact, the accusation of the interlocutor is not correct.

There are several challenges in the automatic annotation of these relations. First, some of the connectors can be ambiguous. In our case, four out of the eight causal discourse connectors in Table 1 are ambiguous (*da, denn, daher* and *darum*) and have, in addition to their causal meaning, temporal, locational or other usages. In example (3), *denn* is used as a particle signaling disbelief, while *daher* is used as a locational verb particle, having, together with the verb 'to come', the interpretation

[2]These examples are taken from the Stuttgart 21 arbitration process, see section 5.1 for more information.

(1) Diese Fahrzeiten sind irrelevant, *da* sie so nicht gefahren werden.
Art.Dem travel time.Pl be.3.Pl irrelevant because they like not drive.Perf.Part be.Fut.3.Pl

Result/Conclusion **Reason**

'These travel times are irrelevant, because they are not executed as specified.'

(2) Das habe ich nicht gesagt, *daher* ist Ihr Vorwurf nicht richtig
Pron have.Pres.1.Sg I not say.Past.Part thus be.3.Sg you.Sg.Pol/Pl accusation not correct

Reason **Result/Conclusion**

'I did not say that, therefore your accusation is not correct.'

(3) Wie kommen Sie *denn daher*?
how come.Inf you.Sg.Pol then VPart
'What is your problem anyway?' (lit. 'In what manner are you coming here?')

(4) *Da* bin ich mir nicht sicher.
there be.Pres.1.Sg I I.Dat not sure
'I'm not sure about that.'

(5) Das kommt *daher*, dass keiner etwas sagt.
Pron come.Pres.3.Sg thus that nobody something say.Pres.3.Sg

Result/Conclusion **Reason**

'This is because nobody says anything.'

of 'coming from somewhere to where the speaker is' (literally and metaphorically). In a second example in (4), *da* is used as the pronominal 'there'.

Second, some of the causal connectors do not always work the same way. In (5), the result/conclusion connector *daher* does not head an embedded clause, rather it is part of the matrix clause. In this case, the embedded clause expresses the reason rather than the result/conclusion. A third challenge is the span of the respective reason and result. While there are some indications as to how to define the stretch of these spans, there are some difficult challenges, further discussed in the error analysis in Section 6.

In the following, we present the rule-based annotation system, which deals with the identification of phrases expressing the result and reason, along the lines illustrated in (1) and (2), as well as with the disambiguation of causal connectors.

4 Rule-based annotation system

The automatic annotation system that we introduce is based on a linguistically informed, handcrafted set of rules that deals with the disambiguation of causal markers and the identification of causal relations in text. As a first step, we divide all of the utterances into smaller units of text in order to be able to work with a more fine-grained structure of the discourse. Following the literature, we call these discourse units. Although there is no consensus in the literature on what exactly a discourse unit consists of, it is generally assumed that each discourse unit describes a single event (Polanyi et al., 2004). Following Marcu (2000), we term these *elementary discourse units* (EDUs) and approximate the assumption made by Polanyi et al. (2004) by inserting a boundary at every punctuation mark and every clausal connector (conjunctions, complementizers). Sentence boundaries are additionally marked.

The annotation of discourse information is performed at the level of EDUs. There are sometimes instances in which a given relation such as "reason" spans multiple EDUs. In these cases, each of the EDUs involved is marked/annotated individually with the appropriate relation.

In the following, we briefly lay out the two elements of the annotation system, namely the disambiguation module and the system for identifying the causal relations.

4.1 Disambiguation

As shown in the examples above, markers like *da, denn, darum* and *daher* 'because/thus' have a number of different senses. The results presented in Dipper and Stede (2006) indicate that POS tagging alone does not help in disambiguating the causal usages from the other functions, particularly not for our data type, which includes much noise and exceptional constructions that are not present in written corpora. As a consequence, we propose a set of rules built on heuristics, which take into account a number of factors in the clause in order to disambiguate the connector. To illustrate the underlying procedure, (6) schematizes part of the disambiguation rule for the German causal connector *da* 'since'.

(6) IF *da* is not followed directly by a verb AND no other particle or connector precedes *da* AND
da is not late in the EDU THEN
da is a causal connector.

In total, the system comprises of 37 rules that disambiguate the causal connectors shown in Table 1. The evaluation in Section 5 shows that the system performs well overall.[3]

4.2 Relation identification

After disambiguation, a second set of rules annotates discourse units as being part of the reason or the result portion of a causal relation. One aspect of deliberation is the assumption that participants in a negotiation justify their positions. Therefore, in this paper, we analyze causal relations within a single utterance of a speaker, i.e., causal relations that are expressed in a sequence of clauses which a speaker utters without interference from another speaker. As a consequence, the annotation system does not take into account causal relations that are split up between utterances of one speaker or utterances of different speakers.

Nevertheless, the reason and result portion of a causal relation can extend over multiple EDUs/sentences and this means that not only EDUs which contain the connector itself are annotated, but preceding/following units that are part of the causal relation also have to be marked. This involves deep linguistic knowledge about the cues that delimit or license relations, information which is encoded in a set of heuristics that feed the 20 different annotation rules and mark the relevant units. An example for a (simplified) relation annotation is given in (7).

(7) IF *result connector* not in first EDU of sentence AND
result connector not preceded by other connector within same sentence THEN
mark every EDU from sentence beginning to current EDU with **reason**.
ELSIF *result connector* in first EDU of sentence THEN
mark every EDU in previous sentence with **reason** UNLESS
encountering another connector.

5 Evaluation

The evaluation is split into two parts. On the one hand, we evaluate the inter-annotator agreement between five, minimally trained annotators (§5.2). On the other hand, we evaluate the rule-based annotation system against this hand-crafted gold-standard (§5.3). Each evaluation is again split into two parts: One concerns the successful identification of the causal connectors. The other concerns the identification of the spans of multilog that indicate a result/conclusion vs. a reason.

5.1 Data

The underlying data comprises of two data sets, the development and the test set. The development set, on which the above-mentioned heuristics for disambiguation and relation identification are based, consists of the transcribed protocols of the Stuttgart 21 arbitration process (henceforth: S21). This public arbitration process took place in 2010

[3]Two reviewers expressed interest in being able to access our full set of rules. Their reasons were two-fold. For one, sharing our rules would benefit a larger community. For another, the reviewers cited concerns with respect to replicability. With respect to the first concern, we will naturally be happy to share our rule set with interested researchers. With respect to the second concern, it is not clear to us that we have understood it. As far as we can tell, what seems to be at the root of the comments is a very narrow notion of replicability, one which involves a freely available corpus in combination with a freely available automatic processing tool (e.g., a machine learning algorithm) that can then be used together without the need of specialist language knowledge. We freely admit that our approach requires specialist linguistic training, but would like to note that linguistic analysis is routinely subject to replicability in the sense that given a set of data, the linguistic analysis arrived at should be consistent across different sets of linguists. In this sense, our work is immediately replicable. Moreover, given the publically available S21 data set and the easily accessible and comprehensive descriptions of German grammar, replication of our work is eminently possible.

and was concerned with a railway and urban development project in the German city of Stuttgart. The project remains highly controversial and has gained international attention. In total, the transcripts contain around 265.000 tokens in 1330 utterances of more than 70 participants.[4]

The test set is based on different, but also transcribed natural speech data, namely on experiments simulating deliberative processes for establishing a governmental form for a hypothetical new African country.[5] For testing, we randomly collected utterances from two versions of the experiment. Each utterance contained at least two causal discourse connectors. In total, we extracted 60 utterances with an average length of 71 words. There are a total of 666 EDUs and 105 instances of the markers in Table 1. The composition of the test set for each (possible) connector is in Table 2.

Reason 'because of'		**Result** 'due to'	
da	23	daher	10
weil	17	darum	11
denn	17	deshalb	12
zumal	4	deswegen	11
Total:	61		44

Table 2: Structure of the evaluation set

For the creation of a gold standard, the test set was manually annotated by two linguistic experts. 238 out of 666 EDUs were marked as being part of the reason of a causal relation, with the result/conclusion contributed by 180 EDUs. Out of 105 connectors found in the test set, 87 have a causal usage. In 18 cases, the markers have other functions.

5.2 Inter-annotator agreement

The task for the annotators comprised of two parts: First, five students (undergraduates in linguistics) had to decide wether an occurence of one of the elements in Table 1 was a causal marker or not. In a second step, they had to mark the boundaries for the reason and result/conclusion parts of the causal relation, based on the boundaries of the automatically generated EDUs. Their annotation choice was not restricted by, e.g., instructing them to choose a 'wider' or more 'narrow' span when in doubt. These tasks served two purposes: On the one hand, we were able to evaluate how easily causal markers can be disambiguated from their other usages and how clearly they introduce either the reason or the result/conclusion of a causal relation. On the other hand, we gained insights into what span of discourse native speakers take to constitute a result/conclusion and cause/reason.

For calculating the inter-annotator agreement (IAA), we used Fleiss' kappa (Fleiss, 1971), which measures the reliability of the agreement between more than two annotators. In the disambiguation task, the annotators' kappa is $\kappa = 0.96$ ("almost perfect agreement"), which shows that the annotators exhibit a high degree of confidence when differentiating between causal and other usages of the markers. When marking whether a connector annotates the reason or the result/conclusion portion of a causal relation, the annotators have a kappa of $\kappa = 0.86$. This shows that not only are annotators capable of reliably disambiguating connectors, they are also reliably labeling each connector with the correct causal relation.

In evaluating the IAA of the spans, we measured three types of relations (reason, result and no causal relation) over the whole utterance, i.e. each EDU which is neither part of the result nor the reason relation was tagged as having no causal relation. We calculated four different κ values: one for each relation type (vs. all other relation types), and one across all relation types. The IAA figures are summarized in Table 3: For the causal relation types, κ_{Reason}=0.86 and κ_{Result}=0.90 indicate near-perfect agreement. κ is significantly higher for causal EDUs than for non-causal (i.e., unmarked) EDUs ($\kappa_{\text{Non-causal}}$=0.82); this is in fact expected since causal EDUs are the marked case and are thus easier to identify for annotators in a coherent manner.

	IAA
κ_{Reason}	0.86
κ_{Result}	0.90
$\kappa_{\text{Non-causal}}$	0.82
κ_{All}	0.73

Table 3: IAA of span annotations

Across all relation types, κ_{All}=0.73 indicates "substantial agreement". The drop in the agreement is anticipated and mirrors the problem that

[4]The transcripts are publicly available for download under `http://stuttgart21.wikiwam.de/Schlichtungsprotokolle`

[5]These have been produced by our collaborators in political science, Katharina Holzinger and Valentin Gold.

is generally found in the literature when evaluating spans of discourse relations (Sporleder and Lascarides, 2008). First, measuring κ_{All} involves three categories, whereas the other measures involve two. Second, a preliminary error analysis shows that there is substantial disagreement regarding the extent of both reason and result spans. The examples in (8)–(9) illustrate this. While annotator 1 marks the result span (indicated by the *(_S* tag) as starting at the beginning of the sentence, annotator 2 excludes the first EDU from the result span.[6] In such cases, we thus register a mismatch in the annotation of the first EDU.

Nevertheless, the numbers indicate a substantial agreement. We thus conclude that the task we set the annotators could be accomplished reliably.

5.3 System performance

In order to evaluate the automatic annotation system described in Section 4, we match the system output against the manually-annotated gold standard, calculating precision, recall and (balanced) f-score of the annotation. For the disambiguation of the connectors in terms of causal versus other usages, the system performs as shown in Table 4 (the ∅ indicates the average of both values).

	Precision	Recall	F-score
Causal	1	0.94	0.97
Non-causal	0.85	1	0.92
∅	**0.93**	**0.97**	**0.95**

Table 4: Causal marker disambiguation

This result is very promising and shows that even though the development data consists of data from a different source, the patterns in the development set are mirrored in the test set. This means that the genre of the spoken exchange of arguments in a multilog does not exhibit the differences usually found when looking at data from different genres, as Mulkar-Mehta et al. (2011a) report when comparing newspaper articles from finance and sport.

For evaluating the annotated spans of reason and result, we base the calculation on whether an EDU is marked with a particular relation or not, i.e. if the system marks an EDU as belonging to the reason or result part of a particular causal marker and the gold standard encodes the same information, then the two discourse units match. As a consequence, spans which do not match perfectly, for example in cases where their boundaries do not match, are not treated as non-matching instances as a whole, but are considered to be made up of smaller units which match individually. Table 5 shows the results.

	Precision	Recall	F-score
Reason	0.88	0.75	0.81
Result	0.81	0.94	0.87
∅	**0.84**	**0.84**	**0.84**

Table 5: Results for relation identification

These results are promising insofar as the detection of spans of causal relations is known to be a problem. Again, this shows that development and test set seem to exhibit similar patterns, despite their different origins (actual political argumentation vs. an experimental set-up). In the following, we present a detailed error analysis and show that we find recurrent patterns of mismatch, most of which can in principle be dealt with quite straightforwardly.

6 Error analysis

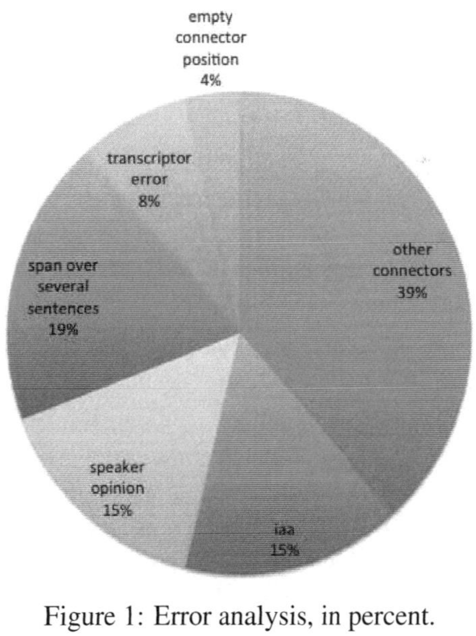

Figure 1: Error analysis, in percent.

Figure 1 shows a pie chart in which each problem is identified and shown with its share in the overall error occurrence. In total, the system makes 26 annotation errors. Starting from the top, *empty connector position* refers to structures which an annotator can easily define as reason/result, but which do not contain an overt connector. This causes the automatic annotation sys-

[6]We use the | sign to indicate EDU boundaries.

(8) Annotator 1:
(_**S** Ich möchte an dieser Stelle einwerfen, | dass die Frage, ob ...
I would like.Pres.1.Sg at this point add.Inf that the question if ...
'I'd like to add at this point that the question if...

(9) Annotator 2:
Ich möchte an dieser Stelle einwerfen, | (_**S** dass die Frage, ob ...
I would like.Pres.1.Sg at this point add.Inf that the question if ...
'I'd like to add at this point that the question if...

tem to fail. The group of *other connectors* refers to cases where a non-causal connector (e.g., the adversative conjunction *aber* 'but') signals the end of the result/conclusion or cause span for a human annotator. The presence of these other connectors and their effect is not yet taken into account by the automatic annotation system. The error group *iaa* refers to the cases where we find a debatable difference of opinion with respect to the length of a span. *Speaker opinion* refers to those cases where a statement starts with expressions like "I believe / I think / in my opinion etc.". These are mostly excluded from a relation span by human annotators, but (again: as of yet) not by the system. *Span over several sentences* refers to those cases where the span includes several sentences. And last, but not least, since the corpus consists of spoken data, an external *transcriptor* had to transcribe the speech signal into written text. Some low-level errors in this category are missing sentence punctuation. The human annotators were able to compensate for this, but not the automatic system.

Roughly, three groups of errors can be distinguished. Some of the errors are relatively easy to solve, by, e.g., adding another class of connectors, by adding expressions or by correcting the transcriptors script. A second group (*span over several sentences* and *empty connector position*) needs a much more sophisticated system, including deep linguistic knowledge on semantics, pragmatics and notoriously difficult aspects of discourse analysis like anaphora resolution.

7 Conclusion

In conclusion, we have presented an automatic annotation system which can reliably and precisely detect German causal relations with respect to eight causal connectors in multilogs in which arguments are exchanged and each party is trying to convince the other of the rightness of their stance. Our system is rule-based and takes into account linguistic knowledge at a similar level as that used by human annotators. Our work will directly benefit research in political science as it can flow into providing one measure for the deliberative quality of a multilog, namely, do interlocutors support their arguments with reasons or not?

References

James Bohman. 1996. *Public Deliberation: Pluralism, Complexity and Democracy.* The MIT Press, Cambridge, MA.

Stefanie Dipper and Manfred Stede. 2006. Disambiguating potential connectives. In *Proceedings of KONVENS (Conference on Natural Language Processing) 2006.*

Quang Xuan Do, Yee Seng Chan, and Dan Roth. 2011. Minimally Supervised Event Causality Identification. In *Proceedings of EMNLP'11*, pages 294–303.

John S. Dryzek. 1990. *Discursive Democracy: Politics, Policy, and Political Science.* Cambridge University Press, Cambridge, MA.

John S. Dryzek. 2000. *Deliberative Democracy and Beyond: Liberals, Critics, Contestations.* Oxford University Press, Oxford.

Joseph L. Fleiss. 1971. Measuring nominal scale agreement among many raters. *Psychological Bulletin*, 76(5):378–382.

Roxana Girju. 2003. Automatic Detection of Causal Relations for Question-Answering. In *Proceedings of the ACL Workshop on Multilingual summarization and question-answering*, pages 76–83.

Amy Gutmann and Dennis Frank Thompson. 1996. *Democracy and Disagreement. Why moral conflict cannot be avoided in politics, and what should be done about it.* Harvard University Press, Cambridge, MA.

Jürgen Habermas. 1981. *Theorie des kommunikativen Handelns.* Suhrkamp, Frankfurt am Main.

Katharina Holzinger and Claudia Landwehr. 2010. Institutional determinants of deliberative interaction. *European Political Science Review*, 2:373–400.

Daniel Marcu. 2000. *The Theory and Practice of Discourse Parsing and Summarization*. MIT Press, Cambridge, Mass.

Rutu Mulkar-Mehta, Andrew S. Gordon, Jerry Hobbs, and Eduard Hovy. 2011a. Causal markers across domains and genres of discourse. In *The 6th International Conference on Knowledge Capture*.

Rutu Mulkar-Mehta, Christopher Welty, Jerry R. Hoobs, and Eduard Hovy. 2011b. Using granularity concepts for discovering causal relations. In *Proceedings of the FLAIRS conference*.

Emily Pitler and Ani Nenkova. 2009. Using syntax to disambiguate explicit discourse connectives in text. In *Proceedings of ACL-IJCNLP*, pages 13–16.

Livia Polanyi, Chris Culy, Martin van den Berg, Gian Lorenzo Thione, and David Ahn. 2004. Sentential structure and discourse parsing. In *Proceedings of the 2004 ACL Workshop on Discourse Annotation*, pages 80–87.

Rashmi Prasad and Aravind Joshi. 2008. A Discourse-based Approach to Generating Why-Questions from Texts. In *Proceedings of the Workshop on the Question Generation Shared Task and Evaluation Challenge*.

Rashmi Prasad, Nikhil Dinesh, Alan Lee, Eleni Miltsakaki, Livio Robaldo, Aravind Joshi, and Bonnie Webber. 2008. The Penn Discourse Treebank 2.0. In *Proceedings of LREC 2008*, pages 2961–2968.

Ted Sanders. 2005. Coherence, Causality and Cognitive Complexity in Discourse. In *Proceedings of SEM-05, First International Symposium on the Exploratiaon and Modelling of Meaning*, pages 105–114.

Angela Schneider and Manfred Stede. 2012. Ambiguity in German Connectives: A Corpus Study. In *Proceedings of KONVENS (Conference on Natural Language Processing) 2012*.

Caroline Sporleder and Alex Lascarides. 2008. Using Automatically Labelled Examples to Classify Rhetorical Relations: An Assessment. *Natural Language Engineering*, 14(3):369–416.

Manfred Stede. 2004. The Potsdam Commentary Corpus. In *In Proceedings of the ACL'04 Workshop on Discourse Annotation*, pages 96–102.

Yannick Versley and Anna Gastel. 2012. Linguistic Tests for Discourse Relations in the Tüba-D/Z Corpus of Written German. *Dialogue and Discourse*, 1(2):1–24.

Yannick Versley. 2010. Discovery of Ambiguous and Unambiguous Discourse Connectives via Annotation Projection. In *Workshop on the Annotation and Exploitation of Parallel Corpora (AEPC)*.

Studying the Semantic Context of two Dutch Causal Connectives

Iris Hendrickx and **Wilbert Spooren**
Centre for Language Studies, Radboud University Nijmegen
P.O. Box 9103, NL-6500 HD Nijmegen The Netherlands
i.hendrickx, w.spooren@let.ru.nl

Abstract

We aim to study the difference of usage between two causal connectives in their semantic context. We present an ongoing study of two Dutch backward causal connectives *omdat* and *want*. Previous linguistic research has shown that causal constructions with *want* are more subjective and often express an opinion. Our hypothesis is that the left and right context surrounding the connectives are more semantically similar in sentences with *omdat* than sentences with *want*. To test this hypothesis we apply two techniques, Latent Semantic Analysis and n-gram overlap. We show that both methods indeed indicate a substantial difference between the two connectives but opposite to what we had expected.

1 Introduction

Much corpus linguistic research has dealt with the issue of subjectivity, i.e. the degree to which the presence of the writer or speaker of a text is felt ((Sanders and Spooren, 2013), and the references cited there). Subjectivity can be located at different levels in a text. At the word level, some words (e.g., evaluative adjectives and expletives) imply a writer/speaker evaluation, whereas others do not. At the sentence level, the description of facts is felt to be more objective, whereas opinions are more subjective. And at the supra-sentential level, subjectivity can get expressed in the type of relation that links the clauses or sentences. For example, argumentative relations are more subjective than statements. Interestingly, many languages make a distinction between more objective or more subjective causal connectives. In Dutch, for example, *omdat* is typically used to express more or less objective backward causal relations, whereas *want* is typically used for more subjective relations. However, these connectives are near synonyms and can be used in the same context as shown in example 1 and 2. There is subtle difference in meaning because example 1 focuses on the reason relation between the two segments whereas 2 focuses on the argument relation. As the first segment is an opinion, *want* is slightly more natural than *omdat*.

(1) Dat is vooral jammer **omdat** de hoofdrolspeler uitstekend zingt.

(2) Dat is vooral jammer **want** de hoofdrolspeler zingt uitstekend.
"That is particularly unfortunate because the protagonist sings excellent."

Note the difference in word order: *want* leads to a coordinative conjunction while *omdat* gives a subordinate conjunction.

We need more insight into this subtle difference between connectives for example to allow natural language generation systems to mimic the choices that native speakers of Dutch make intuitively. Another application would be sentiment analysis where the difference in subjectivity of various connectives can be used to identify subjective or opinionated sentences.

Presently the corpus linguistic analyses of subjective versus objective causal relations have very much been a small-scale enterprise, in that corpus examples were annotated manually. This is problematic for at least two reasons: manual annotation relies on hand coding, with the accompanying problems of poor inter-annotator reliability, and the restricted size of the hand annotated corpora limits the power of statistical generalization. Bestgen et al. (2006) suggested to complement these manual analyses with automatic analyses.

Bestgen and colleagues studied backward causal connections in Dutch. They made use of two types of automatic analyses: Latent Semantic Analysis (LSA) (Deerwester et al., 1990) and what they call Thematic Text Analysis (Popping, 2000) to show that the semantic connection between first and second segment is weaker in a *want* connection than in a *omdat* connection, and that the first segment of *want* connections contains more subjective words than the first segment of *omdat* connections. The materials that were used by Bestgen et al. (2006) were texts from a large corpus of newspaper language of 16.5 million tokens.

The purpose of our current ongoing research project is to extend the automatic analyses in two ways: on the one hand we want to reproduce the LSA analysis of Bestgen et al. using a larger corpus of about 30 million tokens; on the other hand, we want to use n-gram analyses to investigate the semantic connection between the segments in a *want* versus *omdat* connection.

The use of n-grams to measure semantic overlap is a well known method, which has been applied in the standard evaluation metrics for tasks like machine translation and automatic summarization. In these tasks automatic systems aim to produce a text as similar as possible to a manually constructed gold standard text. To evaluate the quality of these automatically produced text, measures such as BLUE (Papineni et al., 2002) and ROUGE (Lin and Hovy, 2003) measure n-gram overlap between the system text and the gold standard text. Furthermore, in other types of research like in the field of literary studies n-grams have been applied, for example to discriminate between genres (Louwerse et al., 2008) or for author discrimination (Hirst and Feiguina, 2007).

Backward causal connectives denotes a cause relation. The connective is positioned in a sentence between the consequence (denoted as Q) and the cause (denoted as P). For the sentence in example 1 Q is the text segment before the connective, and P contains all words after the connective as follows:

Q Dat is vooral jammer

P de hoofdrolspeler uitstekend zingt.

Our hypothesis is that Q and P are more semantically similar in sentences with *omdat* than sentences with *want*. This implies that we expect the average cosine between P and Q to be smaller in *omdat* connections than in *want* connections. We also hypothesize that the number of n-grams shared between P and Q will be higher in *omdat* sentences than in *want* sentences.

This paper presents work in progress. We first describe the SoNaR corpus that was used in this study in section 2. In section 3 we present the experimental setup and results of the experiments with LSA. In section 4 we detail our approach to computing n-grams and we discuss our findings and the next steps to take in 5.

2 Data Collection

Unfortunately neither the corpus nor the data sample used by Bestgen et al. (2006) was available to us. For this reason we chose a similar Duch corpus to work with. The SoNaR corpus (Oostdijk et al., 2013) is a reference corpus of 500 million written words of contemporary Dutch sampled from a wide variety of sources and genres. The corpus has been automatically tokenized, part-of-speech tagged and lemmatized. We took a sample of 100K news articles from the SoNaR corpus as our experimental data set. As we are interested in semantic overlap, we took the lemmatized versions of the articles.

From this data set, we collected all sentences containing the connectives *omdat* and *want*. As we aim to study the semantic relation between Q and P, we only selected sentences that have a meaningful Q and P in the same sentence. We excluded sentences with sentence initial connectives as they only contain a P segment. Sentences with short Q segments (containing one or two words), were manually inspected. A sentence that starts with *dat komt omdat* " this is because" does not contain a meaningful consequence because it refers back to information in a previous sentence. On the other hand, a short Q segment like *tevergeefs, want* "in vain, because" does express a meaningful consequence. In case of sentences with multiple connections, we took the first Q and P and cut off the remainder parts using some handwritten rules. Overall we excluded 20% of *want* sentences and 25% of *omdat* sentences. In total we selected 18,260 for *omdat* and 14,449 sentences for *want*. Some statistics about the sentences is shown in Table 1.

3 LSA

Latent Semantic Analysis (LSA) is a mathematical method for representing word meaning similarity in a semantic space based on a term-by-documents

	Sentences	length	Q len	P len
omdat	18,260	24.3	11.2	12.1
want	14,449	23.5	9.6	12.9

Table 1: Number of sentences and average length in tokens of the full sentence, Q, and P in the data set of *want* and *omdat*.

matrix. It applies singular value decomposition to this matrix to condense it to a smaller semantic representation of around 100 - 500 dimensions (Landauer et al., 1998).

We applied LSA to measure the semantic overlap between Q and P of the *omdat* and *want* sentences. We constructed a term-by-document matrix based on the SoNaR news sample and converted this to an LSA space with 300 dimensions. Each Q and P was projected as a term vector in the LSA space and we computed the cosine similarity between each Q and P.

To build the document-by-term matrix for LSA, words were lemmatized, and punctuation, digits and stopwords (based on a stopword list of 221 words) were filtered out.

In our first analysis we used the top most frequent words that occurred at least 15 times, leading to a text matrix of approximately 20,000 documents and 19,000 word terms. We calculated the cosine between Q and P for each of the *omdat* and *want* sequences. A Welch Two Sample t-test showed that contrary to expectation the cosine between Q and P was lower for *omdat* (0.039) than for *want* (0.045; $t(29518)=-4.78$, $p < .001$).

In a second analysis we chose a sample of a different scale and we used a text matrix of 100,000 documents and the top 10,000 most frequent word terms. A t-test showed that in this case the cosine for *omdat* sequences was slightly but significantly higher than for *want* sequences (*omdat*: 0.048; *want*: 0.043; $t(30175)=3.68$, $p < .001$).

In the final section we will go into possible explanations for these unexpected and incompatible results.

4 N-gram overlap

In our study of n-grams, we looked both at pure bigram statistics and at n-grams in a broader scope, i.e. n-grams and skip-grams with a maximal length of 10 tokens. All n-grams have a minimum length of 2, and a minimum frequency of 2 in the datasample. We use lemmatized words to reduce the influence of morphological information. For the n-gram analysis we used the Colibri software package developed by Maarten van Gompel[1] (van Gompel, 2014). In the left part of Table 2 we show the bigram statistics and on the right side the n-gram statistics of n-grams that occur at least twice in Q, P, and those occurring in both Q and P. We present the following counts:

- Pattern - The number of distinct n-gram patterns (n-gram type count)
- Coverage - The number of unigram word tokens covered as a fraction of the total number of unigram tokens.
- Occurrences - Cumulative occurrence count of all the patterns (n-gram token count).

We can observe that about 75% of the tokens in Q and P is covered in this bigram analysis, while the n-grams cover around 93% of the words. Zooming in on the bigrams and n-grams that are shared in Q and P, we can see that these cover about 50% and 75% of the tokens respectively. This shows that we can safely discard n-grams that occur only once in our counts and still cover most tokens in the data sample.

Based on the bigram occurrences in our data set, we computed whether the bigram overlap between Q and P in *omdat* sentences is larger than in *want* sentences. We used a loglikelihood test to compare the relative frequencies as our samples do not have the same size. We found that 72362 bigram occurrences (or 67.8%) overlap in *omdat* sentences and 58213 bigrams (or 79.4%) for *want* sentences ($LL2(1)=808.40$, $p < .01$). This means that, contrary to our hypothesis, we found more overlap for *want* sentences.

We performed the same computation on the larger set of n-grams. We saw that 81573 of n-gram occurrences (44.9%) overlap in *omdat* sentences and 65272 (51.1%) overlap in for *want* sentences ($LL2(1)=595.37$, $p < .01$). This then is again a confirmation that we find more overlap between Q and P in *want* sentences.

5 Conclusions

In this paper we report two types of automatic analyses of the differences between *want* and *om-*

[1] available at: http://proycon.github.io/colibri-core/

Category	Bigrams			n-grams		
	Patterns	Coverage	Occurrences	Patterns	Coverage	Occurrences
omdat Q	18931	0.7312	106766	39780	0.9320	181506
omdat P	20649	0.7549	118414	45074	0.9380	208809
omdat Q&P	7261	0.5042	72362	9213	0.8927	81573
want Q	12938	0.7474	73276	27654	0.9350	127723
want P	17564	0.7216	94685	37027	0.9271	159125
want Q&P	5774	0.4847	58213	7365	0.7943	65272

Table 2: Counts of the bigrams and n-grams up to length 10 with minimal frequency 2 in Q, P, and those n-grams that occur in both Q and P. Patterns refers to n-gram types, Occurrences to n-gram tokens and Coverage refers to word token coverage.

dat, which have been claimed to differ in subjectivity, i.e. the degree to which the writer is felt present in the text. One part of our study is a reproduction of (Bestgen et al., 2006) and assessed the semantic relationship between Q and P in terms of a LSA cosine for *want* and *omdat*. Contrary to the findings of Bestgen et al., our first LSA analysis showed that the relationship between Q and P is less strong for *omdat* than for *want*. A second analysis found a small difference in the expected direction. In the second part of our study we used n-gram overlap as a different type of similarity measure. Again, our hypothesis was not borne out in that *omdat* showed a significantly smaller degree of overlap than *want*.

At this moment we cannot explain why the two LSA experiments presented in section 3 show significant results in different directions. In the two experiments the same connective sentences were used, but the semantic space in which they were projected was different. For our LSA analysis we made use of the software package LSA in R. To rule out the possibility that our results were due to some implementation peculiarity, we ran a small test sample with another LSA implementation Gensim (Řehůřek and Sojka, 2010). Both implementations gave us similar cosine values for the same sample.

A noticeable difference with the Bestgen et al. study is the size of the cosines: Bestgen et al. report mean cosines of 0.120 and 0.137 for *want* and *omdat*, respectively, whereas in our study we found mean cosines of 0.045 and 0.039, respectively. This suggests that our data sample and experimental setup differ substantially from the work of Bestgen et al. and we did not succeed in reproducing their experiment. In our analysis the semantic relationship between Q and P is much weaker.

In order to be able to interpret these results, we added a baseline experiment. Here we ran an LSA experiment with segments composed of random words of the exact same size for the *omdat* and *want* sentences. For *omdat* this gave us a mean cosine similarity of 0.007 and for *want* 0.006. This implies that the cosines we found are significantly higher than comparing random strings of words.

Note that the analysis was carried out on a sufficiently large corpus and sufficient numbers of occurrences of *want* and *omdat*. Moreover, the result that semantic relationship is stronger in *want* than in *omdat* is corroborated by our n-gram analysis.

One possible explanation of the results of the n-gram analysis is the syntactic difference between *want* and *omdat* sentences. In *want* sentences the word order of Q and P is the same while for *omdat* the verb-predicate order is swapped. The n-grams will pick up this difference. As a next step we plan to run the n-gram analysis with alphabetically ordered n-grams to exclude the effect of this syntactic difference[2].

Another line of future research is to make genre comparisons. The availability of the SoNaR corpus makes it possible to investigate the subjectivity hypothesis for different text genres.

Finally we intend to follow up our analysis with a machine learning experiment to investigate whether a learner could distinguish a *want* sentence from a *omdat* sentence by looking at a local context window of words to automatically predict *want* or *omdat*.

[2]We wish to thank one of our anonymous reviewers for bringing this suggestion to our attention.

References

Yves Bestgen, Liesbeth Degand, and Wilbert Spooren. 2006. Toward automatic determination of the semantics of connectives in large newspaper corpora. *Discourse Processes*, 41(2):175–193.

Scott C. Deerwester, Susan T Dumais, Thomas K. Landauer, George W. Furnas, and Richard A. Harshman. 1990. Indexing by latent semantic analysis. *Journal of the American Society for Information Science*, 41(6):391–407.

Graeme Hirst and Olga Feiguina. 2007. Bigrams of syntactic labels for authorship discrimination of short texts. *Literary and Linguistic Computing*, 22(4):405–417.

Thomas K Landauer, Peter W Foltz, and Darrell Laham. 1998. An introduction to latent semantic analysis. *Discourse processes*, 25(2-3):259–284.

C.-Y. Lin and E.H. Hovy. 2003. Automatic evaluation of summaries using n-gram co-occurrence statistics. In *Proceedings of the Human Language Technology Conference of the North American Chapter of the Association for Computational Linguistics (HLT-NAACL)*, pages 71 – 78, Edmonton, Canada.

Max Louwerse, Nick Benesh, and Bin Zhang, 2008. *Directions in Empirical Literary Studies: In honor of Willie van Peer*, chapter Computationally discriminating literary from non-literary texts, pages 175–191. John Benjamins Publishing.

Nelleke Oostdijk, Martin Reynaert, Véronique Hoste, and Ineke Schuurman. 2013. The construction of a 500-million-word reference corpus of contemporary written dutch. In *Essential Speech and Language Technology for Dutch*, pages 219–247. Springer.

Kishore Papineni, Salim Roukos, Todd Ward, and Wei jing Zhu. 2002. BLEU: a Method for Automatic Evaluation of Machine Translation. pages 311–318.

R. Popping. 2000. *Computer-assisted text analysis*. Sage, London.

Radim Řehůřek and Petr Sojka. 2010. Software Framework for Topic Modelling with Large Corpora. In *Proceedings of the LREC 2010 Workshop on New Challenges for NLP Frameworks*, pages 45–50, Valletta, Malta, May. ELRA.

T.J.M. Sanders and W.P.M.S. Spooren. 2013. Exceptions to rules: a qualitative analysis of backward causal connectives in Dutch naturalistic discourse. *Text & Talk*, 33(3):399–420.

Maarten van Gompel, 2014. *Colibri Documentation, Colibri Core 0.1*. Centre for Language Studies, Radboud University Nijmegen, The Netherlands. http://proycon.github.io/colibri-core/doc/.

Building a Japanese Corpus of Temporal-Causal-Discourse Structures Based on SDRT for Extracting Causal Relations

Kimi Kaneko [1] **Daisuke Bekki** [1,2,3]
[1] Ochanomizu University, Tokyo, Japan
[2] National Institute of Informatics, Tokyo, Japan
[3] CREST, Japan Science and Technology Agency, Saitama, Japan
{kaneko.kimi | bekki}@is.ocha.ac.jp

Abstract

This paper proposes a methodology for generating specialized Japanese data sets for the extraction of causal relations, in which temporal, causal and discourse relations at both the fact level and the epistemic level, are annotated. We applied our methodology to a number of text fragments taken from the Balanced Corpus of Contemporary Written Japanese. We evaluated the feasibility of our methodology in terms of agreement and frequencies, and discussed the results of the analysis.

1 Introduction

In recent years, considerable attention has been paid to deep semantic processing. Many studies (Betherd et al., 2008), (Inui et al., 2007), (Inui et al., 2003), (Riaz and Girju, 2013) have been recently conducted on deep semantic processing, and causal relation extraction (CRE) is one of the specific tasks in deep semantic processing. Research on CRE is still developing and there are many obstacles that must be overcome.

Inui *et al.* (2003) acquired cause and effect pairs from text, where the antecedent events were taken as causes and consequent events were taken as effects based on Japanese keywords such as *kara* and *node*. In (1), for example, the antecedent *ame-ga hutta* ('it rained') and the consequent *mizutamari-ga dekita* ('puddles emerged') are acquired as a pair of cause and effect.

(1) Ame-ga hutta-*node*
rain-NOM fall-past-*because*
mizutamari-ga dekita.
puddles-NOM emerge-past
'Because it rained, puddles emerged.'

However, antecedents are not always causes or reasons for consequents in Japanese, as illustrated by the following example.

(2) Zinsinziko-ga
injury.accident-NOM
okita-*kara* densya-ga
happen-past-*because* trains-NOM
tiensita to-iu-wake-dewanai.
delay-past it.is.not.the.case.that
'It is not the case that the trains were delayed because an injury accident happened.'

In example (2), the antecedent *zinsinziko-ga okita* ('an injury accident happened') is not the cause of the consequent *densya-ga tiensita* ('the trains were delayed'). Though in such sentences that contain causal expressions there are no causal relations between antecedents and consequents, in existing studies each sentence containing a causal expression was extracted as knowledge representing cause and effect, such as in (Inui et al., 2003). It is difficult for computers to auto-recognize and exclude such cases.

In this paper, we report on the analysis of necessary information for acquiring more accurate cause-effect knowledge and propose a methodology for creating a Japanese corpus for CRE. First, we introduce previous studies and describe information that should be used to annotate data sets. Next, we describe our methodology based on Segmented Discourse Representation Theory (SDRT) (Asher et al., 2003). Finally, we evaluate the validity of our methodology in terms of agreement and frequency, and analyze the results.

2 Previous Studies

In this section, we introduce previous studies on annotation of temporal, causal and other types of relations and present a linguistic analysis of temporal and causal relations.

Betherd *et al.* (2008) generated English data sets annotated with temporal and causal relations and analyzed interactions between the two types of relations. In addition, these specialized data sets were evaluated in terms of agreement and accuracy. Relations were classified into two causal categories (CAUSAL, NO-REL) and three temporal categories (BEFORE, AFTER, NO-REL). In regard to the evaluation, Betherd *et al.* pointed out that the classification was coarse-grained, and that reanalysis would have to be performed with more fine-grained relations.

Inui *et al.* (2005) characterized causal expressions in Japanese text and built Japanese corpus with tagged causal relations. However, usages such as that illustrated in (2) and interactions between temporal relations and causal relations were not analyzed.

Tamura (2012) linguistically analyzed temporal and causal relations and pointed out that in reason/purpose constructions in Japanese, the event time indicated by the tense sometimes contradicts the actual event time, and that the information necessary to recognize the order between events lies in the choice of the *fact* and the *epistemic* levels (we will come back to these notions in the section 3.4), and the explicit or implicit meaning of a sentence in the causal expressions in Japanese. Furthermore, some causal expressions in Japanese are free from the absolute and relative tense systems, and both the past and non-past forms can be freely used in main and subordinate clauses (Chin, 1984) (an example is given in the next section). In other words, temporal relations are not always resolved earlier than causal relations, and therefore we should resolve temporal relations and causal relations simultaneously.

Asher *et al.* (2003) proposed SDRT in order to account for cases where discourse relations affect the truth condition of sentences. Because temporal relations constrain causal relations, the explicit or implicit meaning of a sentences and the epistemic level information affects preceding and following temporal relations in causal expressions in Japanese, recognition also affects causal relations. Therefore, the annotation of both causal relations and discourse relations in corpora is expected to be useful for CRE. Moreover, which characteristics (such as tense, actual event time, time when the event is recognized, meaning and structure of the sentence and causal relations) will serve as input and which of them will serve as output depends on the time and place. Therefore, we should also take into account discourse relations together with temporal and causal relations. We can create specialized data sets for evaluating these types of information together by annotating text with discourse, temporal and causal relations.

However, discourse relations of SDRT are not distributed into discourse relations and temporal relations, and as a result the classification of labels becomes unnecessarily complex. Therefore, it is necessary to rearrange discourse relations as in the following example.

(3) Inu-wa niwa-o kakemawatta.
dog-NOM garden-ACC run-past
Neko-wa $kotatu$-de
cat-NOM $kotatsu$.heater-LOC
marukunatte-ita.
be.curled.up-past
'The dog ran in the garden. The cat was curled up in the *kotatsu* heater.'

This pair of sentences is an antithesis, so we annotate it with the "Contrast" label in SDRT. On the other hand, the situation described in the first sentence overlaps with that of the second sentence, so we annotate this pair of sentences with the "Background" label as well. Though there are many cases in which we can annotate a sentence with discourse relations in this way, dividing temporal relations from discourse relations as in this study allows us to avoid overlapping discourse relations.

This study was performed with the aim to rearrange SDRT according to discourse relations, temporal relations and causal relations separately, and we generated specialized data sets according to our methodology. In addition, occasionally it is necessary to handle the actual event time and the time when the event was recognized individually. An example is given below.

(4) Asu tesuto-ga
tomorrow exam-NOM
aru-<u>node</u>, kyoo-wa
take.place-nonpast-<u>*because*</u>, today-TOP
benkyoo-suru-koto-ni sita.
to.study-DAT decide-past
'Because there will be an exam tomorrow, I decided to study today.

Before we evaluate the consequent *kyoo-wa benkyoo-suru-koto-ni sita* ('I decided to study today'), we should recognize the fact of the antecedent *Asu tesuto-ga aru* ('there will be an exam tomorrow'). Whether we deal with the actual

Label	Description
Precedence(A,B)	End time (A) < start time (B) In other words, event A temporally precedes event B.
Overlap(A,B)	Start time (A) < end time (B) ≤ end time (B) < end time (A), In other words, event A temporally overlaps with event B.
Subsumption(A,B)	Start time (A) ≤ end time (B) & End time (A) ≤ end time (B), In other words, event A temporally subsumes event B.

Table 1: Temporal relations list

Level	Description
Cause(A,B)	The event in A and the event in B are in a causal relation.

Table 2: Causal relation

event time or the time when the event was recognized depends on the circumstances. Therefore, we decided to annotate text at the fact and epistemic levels in parallel to account for such a distinction.

3 Methodology

We extended and refined SDRT and developed our own methodology for annotating main and subordinate clauses, phrases located between main and subordinate clauses (e.g., continuative conjuncts in Japanese), two consecutive sentences and two adjoining nodes with a discourse relation. We also defined our own method for annotating propositions with causal and temporal relations. The result of tagging example (5a) is shown in (5b).

(5) a. Kaze-ga huita. Harigami-ga
wind-NOM blow-past poster-NOM
hagare, tonda.
come.off-past flow-past

'The wind blew. A poster came off and flew away.'

b. **[Precedence($\pi 1$,$\pi 3$),Explanation($\pi 1$,$\pi 3$), Cause($\pi 1$,$\pi 3$)], [Precedence($\pi 2$,$\pi 4$), Explanation($\pi 2$,$\pi 4$), Cause($\pi 2$,$\pi 4$)]**
$_{\pi 2 \pi 1}$Kaze-ga huita.
$_{\pi 4 \pi 3}$Harigami-ga hagare, tonda.

The remainder of this section is structured as follows. Sections 3.1 and 3.2 deal with temporal and causal relations, respectively. Section 3.3 covers discourse relations, and Section 3.4 describes the fact level and the epistemic level.

3.1 Temporal Relations

We consider the following three temporal relations (Table 1). We assume that they represent the relations between two events in propositions and indicate a start time and an end time. In addition, we also assume that (start time of e) $\leq$ (end time of e) for all events. Based on this, the temporal placement of each two events is limited to the three relations in Table 1.

In this regard, Japanese non-past predicates occasionally express habitually repeating events, which have to be distinguished from events occurring later than the reference point. In this paper, in annotating the scope of the repetition, habitually repeating events are described as in the following example.

(6) a. Taiin-go, {kouen-o
After.retirement park-ACC
hasiru}$_{repeat}$ yoo-ni-site-iru.
to.run have.a.custom

'After retiring, I have a custom to {run in the park}$_{repeat}$.'

b. {supootu-inryo-o nonda-ato,
Sports.drink-ACC drink-past-after
kouen-o hasiru}$_{repeat}$
park-ACC run
yoo-ni-site-iru.
have.a.custom

'I have a custom that {I run in the park after having a sports drink}$_{repeat}$.'

3.2 Causal Relations

We tag pairs of clauses with the following relation (Table 2) only if there is a causal relation between events in the proposition. By annotating text with discourse relations, a fact and epistemic level and temporal relations, we can describe the presence

Label	Description
Alternation(A,B)	"A or B", where the pair of A and B corresponds to logical disjunction ($\vee$).
Consequence(A,B)	"If A then B", where the pair of A and B corresponds to logical implication ($\rightarrow$).
Elaboration(A,B)	B explains A in detail in the discourse relation. B of the event is part of A of the event.
Narration(A,B)	A and B are in the same situation, and the pair of A and B corresponds to logical conjunction ($\wedge$).
Explanation(A,B)	The discourse relation indicates A as a cause and B as an effect.
Contrast(A,B)	"A but B", where A and B are paradoxical.
Commentary(A,B)	The content of A is summarized or complemented in B.

Table 3: Discourse relations list

SDRT	Our methodology	Rules
Alternation(A,B)	Alternation(A,B)	NA
Consequence(A,B)	Consequence(A,B)	NA
Elaboration(A,B)	Elaboration(A,B)	$\forall$ A,B (Elaboration(A,B) $\rightarrow$ Subsumption (A,B))
Narration(A,B)	Precedence(A,B) $\wedge$ Narration(A,B)	NA
Background(A,B)	Subsumption(A,B) $\wedge$ Narration(A,B)	NA
Result(A,B) **Explanation(A,B)**	Explanation(A,B) Cause(A,B)	 $\forall$ A,B (Cause(A,B) $\rightarrow$ Temp_rel(A,B)) [1]
Contrast(A,B)	Contrast(A,B)	NA
Commentary(A,B)	Commentary(A,B)	NA

Table 4: Correspondence between SDRT and our methodology

of causation in finer detail than (Betherd et al., 2008).

3.3 Discourse Relations

We consider the following discourse relations based on SDRT (Table 3). There are also relations that impose limitations on temporal and causal relations (Table 4). The way temporal, causal and discourse relations affect each other is described below together with their correspondence to the relations in SDRT. **Bold-faced** entries represent relations integrated in SDRT in our study.
Such limitations on temporal relations provides information for making a decision in terms of temporal order and cause/effect in the "de-tensed" sentence structure [2] (Chin, 1984) in Japanese. An example is given below.

(7) Kinoo anna-ni taberu-*kara*,
yesterday that.much eat-past-*because*
kyoo onaka-ga itaku
today stomach-NOM ache-cont
natta-nda.
become-*noda*

'Because you ate that much yesterday, you have a stomachache today.'

(7) **[Precedence($\pi1$,$\pi3$),Explanation($\pi1$,$\pi3$), Cause($\pi1$,$\pi3$)], [Precedence($\pi2$,$\pi4$),Explanation($\pi2$,$\pi4$), Cause($\pi2$,$\pi4$)]**
$_{\pi2\pi1}$Kinoo anna-ni taberu-*kara*,
$_{\pi4\pi3}$kyoo onaka-ga itaku natta-nda.

This is a sentence where the subordinate clause is in non-past tense and the main clause is in past tense. Then, we may mistakenly interpret the event in the subordinate clause as occurring after the event of the main clause. However, we can determine that in fact it occurred *before* the event in the main clause based on the rule imposed by the "Cause" relation.

3.4 Fact Level and Epistemic Level

A fact level proposition refers to an event and its states, while an epistemic level proposition refers to speaker's *recognizing* event of a described event. In Japanese, the latter form is often marked by the suffix *noda* that attaches to all kinds of predicates (which may also be omitted). Both overt and covert *noda* introduce embedded structures, and we annotate them in such a way that a fact level proposition is embedded in an epistemic level proposition.

Semantically, the most notable difference between the two levels is that the tense in the former

[2] Temp_rel(A,B) $\equiv$ Precedence(A,B)$\vee$ Overlap(A,B) $\vee$ Subsumption(A,B)

[3] According to (Chin, 1984), "de-tensed" is a relation whereby the phrase has lost the meaning contributed by tense, namely, the logical aspect of the semantic relation between an antecedent and a consequent has eliminated the aspect temporal relation between them.

represents the time that an event takes place, while the tense in the latter represents the time that the speaker *recognizes* the event.

This distinction between the two types of propositions is carried over to the distinction between the fact level and the epistemic level causal relations. We annotate the former by the tag "Cause" and the latter by the tag "Explanation".

In Japanese, a causal marker such as *node* (a continuation form of *noda*) and *kara* are both used in the fact level and the epistemic level. The fact level causality is a causal relation between the two events, while the epistemic level causality is a causal relation between the two *recognizing* events of the two events mentioned. Therefore, in the causal construction, it happens that the precedence relations between the subordinate and the matrix clauses in the fact level and the epistemic level do not coincide, as in the following example.

(8) Kesa nani-mo
this.morning nothing-NOM
hoodoo-sare-nakatta-*node*,
report-passive-NEG.past-*because*,
kinoo-wa mebosii ziken-wa
yesterday-TOP notable events-NOM
nakatta-noda.
be-NEG-*noda*
'Because nothing was reported this morning, there were no notable event yesterday.'

[Precedence(π3,π1),Explanation(π3,π1), Cause(π3,π1)], [Precedence(π2,π4), Explanation(π2,π4), Cause(π2,π4)]

$_{\pi 2 \pi 1}$Kesa nani-mo hoodoo-sare-nakatta-*node*, $_{\pi 4 \pi 3}$kinoo-wa mebosii ziken-wa nakatta-noda.

The temporal relation at the fact level is that π3 precedes π1. By contrast, that at the epistemic level is that π2 precedes π4. By describing the relation between π1 and π3 and that between π2 and π4 separately, we can reproduce the relationship at both levels.

3.5 Merits

We defined our methodology for annotating text fragments at both the fact and epistemic levels in parallel with temporal, causal and discourse relations. Therefore, we can generate specialized data sets that enable estimating the causality in the fact and epistemic levels by various cues (such as known causal relations, truth condition, conjunctions and temporal relations between sentences or clauses).

In addition, we can say that causal expressions without causation are not in a causal relation (and vice versa) by annotating text with both discourse and causal relations.

4 Results

We applied our methodology to 66 sentences from the Balanced Corpus of Contemporary Written Japanese (BCCWJ) (Maekawa, 2008). The sentences were decomposed by one annotator, and labels were assigned to the decomposed segments by two annotators. During labeling, we used the labels presented in Section 3. Our methodology was developed based on 96 segments (38 sentences), and by using the other 100 segments (28 sentences), we evaluated the inter-annotator agreement as well as the frequencies of decomposition and times of annotation. The agreement for 196 segments generated from 28 sentences amounted to 0.68 and was computed as follows (the kappa coefficient for them amounted to 0.79).

$$Agreement = Agreed\ labels / Total\ labels$$

Analyzing more segments in actual text and improving our methodology can lead to further improvement in terms of agreement.

Table 5 shows the distribution of labels into segments in our study.

label	**segments**		
	Total	fact	epistemic
Precedence	25	14	11
Overlap	7	4	3
Subsumption	61	29	32
total	**94**	**47**	**47**
Cause	14	8	6
total	**14**	**8**	**6**
Alternation	–	–	–
Consequence	6	3	3
Elaboration	4	2	2
Narration	66	33	33
Explanation	14	7	7
Contrast	2	1	1
Commentary	**94**	**47**	**47**

Table 5: Distribution of labels in segments in our study

We can see from Table 5 that "Narration" was the most frequent one, while "Alternation" never appeared. As s result, we can assume that frequent relations will be separated from non-frequent relations. So far, all the relations are either frequent or non-frequent. We should re-analyze the data with more samples again.

When the methodology was applied to 28 sentences, a total of 100 and an average of 3.57 segments were derived. This is the number of segments at both the fact and epistemic levels. Without dividing the fact and epistemic levels, an average of 1.79 segments were derived.

On average, 11 segments per hour were tagged in our study. Although we should evaluate the validity after having computed the average decomposition times, it is assumed that our methodology is valid when focusing only on labeling.

5 Discussion

We analyzed errors in this annotation exercise. The annotators often found difficulties in judging temporal relations in the following two cases: (1) the case where it was difficult to determine the scope of the segments pairing and (2) the case where formalization of lexical meaning is difficult.

In regard to the first case, how to divide segments sometimes affects temporal relations. In the following example, consider the temporal relation between the first and the second sentences.

(9) Marason-ni syutuzyoo-sita.
marathon-DAT participate-past.
sonohi-wa 6zi-ni kisyoo-si,
that.day-TOP 6:00-at get.up-past,
10zi-ni totyoo-kara
10:00-at Metropolitan.Government-from
syuppatu-site, 12zi-ni
leave-past, 12:00-at
kansoo-sita.
finish.running-past.
'I participated in marathon. I got up at 6:00 on that day and left the Metropolitan Government at 10:00 and finished running at 12:00.'

When we focus on the first segment of the second sentnce (*'I got up at 6:00'*), its relation to the first sentence appears to be "Precedence". However, if we consider the second and the third segments as the same segment, their relation to the first sentence appears to be "Subsumption".

Therefore, we should establish clear criteria for the segmentation. Although we currently adopts a criterion that we chose smaller segment in unclear cases, there still remain 9 unclear cases (temporal:5, discourse:4).

One of the reason why Kappa coefficient marks relatively high score is that we only compare the labels and ignore the difference in the segmentations. Criteria for deciding the segment scope in paring segments will improve our methodology.

The second case is exemplified by the temporal relation between the subordinate clause and the main clause in the following sentence.

(10) Migawari-no tomo-o
scapegoat-GEN friend-ACC
sukuu-*tame-ni* hasiru-noda.
to.save run-*noda*.
'I run to save my friend who is my scapegoat.'

If we consider that the *saving* event only spans over the very moment of *saving*, the relation between the clauses appears to be "Precedence". However, if we consider that *running* event is a part of the *saving* event, the relation between the clauses is "Subsumption".

Thus, judging lexical meaning with respect to when events start and end involves some difficulties and they yield delicate cases in judging temporal relations.

These problems are mutually related, and the first problem arises when the components of a lexical meaning are displayed explicitly in the sentence, and the second problem arises when they are implicit.

6 Conclusions

We analyzed and proposed our methodology based on SDRT for building a more precise Japanese corpus for CRE. In addition, we annotated 196 segments (66 sentences) in BCCWJ with temporal relations, discourse relations, causal relations and fact level and epistemic level propositions and evaluated the annotations of 100 segments (28 sentences) in terms of agreement, frequencies and times for decompositions. We reported and analyzed the result and discussed problems of our methodology.

The discrepancies of decomposition patterns were not yet empirically compared in the present study and will be investigated in future work.

References

Asher N. and Lascaridas A. 2003. *Logics of Conversation: Studies in Natural Language Processing*. Cambridge University Press, Cambridge, UK.

Bethard S., Corvey W. and Kilingenstein S. 2008. *Building a Corpus of Temporal Causal Structure*. LREC 2008, Marrakech, Morocco.

Chin M. 1984. *Tense of the predicates for clauses of compound statement binded by conjunctive particle -"Suru-Ga" and "Shita-Ga", "Suru-Node" and "Shita-Node" etc.-*. Language Teaching Research Article.

Inui T., Inui K. and Matsumoto Y. 2005. *Acquiring Causal Knowledge from Text Using the Connective Marker Tame*. ACM Transactions on Asian Language Information Processing (ACM-TALIP), Vol.4, Issue 4, Special Issue on Recent Advances in Information Processing and Access for Japanese, 435–474.

Inui T., Inui K. and Matsumoto Y. 2003. *What Kinds and Amounts of Causal Knowledge Can Be Aquired from Text by Using Connective Markers as Clues*. The 6th International Conference on Discovery Science (DS-2003), 180–193.

Inui T., Takamura H. and Okumura M. 2007. *Latent Variable Models for Causal Knowledge Acquisition. Alexander Gelbukh(Ed.), Computational Linguistics and Intelligent Text Processing, Lecture Notes in Computer Science*, 4393:85–96.

Maekawa K. 2008. *Balanced Corpus of Contemporary Written Japanese*. In Proceedings of the 6th Workshop on Asian Language Resources (ALR), 101—102.

Riaz M. and Girju R. 2013. *Toward a Better Understanding of Causality between Verbal Events:Extraction and Analysis of the Causal Power of Verb-Verb Associations*. In Proceedings of the SIGDIAL 2013 Conference, Metz, France 21–30.

Tamura S. 2012. *Causal relations and epistemic perspectives: Studies on Japanese causal and purposive constructions*. Doctoral thesis, Kyoto University.

Likelihood of external causation in the structure of events

Tanja Samardžić
CorpusLab, URPP Language and Space
University of Zurich
tanja.samardzic@uzh.ch

Paola Merlo
Linguistics Department
University of Geneva
Paola.Merlo@unige.ch

Abstract

This article addresses the causal structure of events described by verbs: whether an event happens spontaneously or it is caused by an external causer. We automatically estimate the likelihood of external causation of events based on the distribution of causative and anticausative uses of verbs in the causative alternation. We train a Bayesian model and test it on a monolingual and on a bilingual input. The performance is evaluated against an independent scale of likelihood of external causation based on typological data. The accuracy of a two-way classification is 85% in both monolingual and bilingual setting. On the task of a three-way classification, the score is 61% in the monolingual setting and 69% in the bilingual setting.

1 Introduction

Ubiquitously present in human thinking, causality is encoded in language in various ways. Computational approaches to causality are mostly concerned with automatic extraction of causal schemata (Michotte, 1963; Tversky and Kahneman, 1982; Gilovich et al., 1985) from spontaneously produced texts based on linguistic encoding. A key to success in this endeavour is understanding how human language encodes causality.

Linguistic expressions of causality, such as causative conjunctions, verbs, morphemes, and constructions, are highly ambiguous, encoding not only the real-world causality, but also the structure of discourse, as well as speakers' attitudes (Moeschler, 2011; Zufferey, 2012). Causality judgements are hard to elicit in an annotation project. This results in a low inter-annotator agreement and makes the evaluation of automatic systems difficult (Bethard, 2007; Grivaz, 2012).

Our study addresses the relationship between world-knowledge about causality and the grammar of language, focusing on the causal structure of events expressed by verbs. In current analyses, the meaning of verbs is decomposed into multiple predicates which can be in a temporal and causal relation (Pustejovsky, 1995; Talmy, 2000; Levin and Rappaport Hovav, 2005; Ramchand, 2008).

(1) a. *Causative*: Adam broke the laptop.
b. *Anticausative*: The laptop broke.

We propose a computational approach to the *causative alternation*, illustrated in (1), in which an event (*breaking the laptop* in (1)) can be dissociated from its immediate causer (*Adam* in (1a)). The causative alternation has been attested in almost all languages (Schafer, 2009), but it is realised with considerable cross-linguistic variation in the sets of alternating verbs and in the grammatical encoding (Alexiadou et al., 2006; Alexiadou, 2010).

Since the causative alternation involves most verbs, identifying the properties of verbs which allow them to alternate is important for developing representations of the meaning of verbs in general. Analysing the structural components of the meaning of verbs proves important for tasks such as word sense disambiguation (Lapata and Brew, 2004), semantic role labelling (Màrquez et al., 2008), cross-linguistic transfer of semantic annotation (Padó and Lapata, 2009; Fung et al., 2007; van der Plas et al., 2011). The knowledge about the likelihood of external causation might be helpful in the task of detecting implicit arguments of verbs and, especially deverbal nouns (Gerber and Chai, 2012; Roth and Frank, 2012). Knowing, for example, that a verb expresses an externally caused event increases the probability of an implicit causer if an explicit causer is not detected in a particular instance of the verb. Our study should contribute to the development of formal and extensive representations of grammatically relevant semantic properties of verbs, such as Verb Net (Kipper Schuler, 2005) and PropBank (Palmer et al., 2005).

2 External Causation and the Grammar of Language

The distinction between external and internal causation in events described by verbs is introduced by Levin and Rappaport Hovav (1994) to account for the fact that the alternation is blocked in some verbs such as *bloom* in (2). In Levin and Rappaport Hovav's account, verbs which describe externally caused events alternate (1), while verbs which describe internally caused events do not (2).

(2) a. The flowers suddenly bloomed.
b. * The summer bloomed the flowers.

The main objection to this proposed generalisation is that it does not account for the cross-linguistic variation. Since the distinction concerns the meaning of verbs, one could expect that the verbs which are translations of each other alternate in all languages. This is, however, often not true. There are many verbs that do alternate in some languages, while their counterparts in other languages do not (Alexiadou et al., 2006; Schafer, 2009; Alexiadou, 2010). For example, *appear* and *arrive* do not alternate in English, but their equivalents in Japanese or in the Salish languages do.

To account for the variation in cross-linguistic data Alexiadou (2010) introduces the notion of cause-unspecified events, a category between externally caused and internally caused events. Introducing gradience into the classification allows Alexiadou to propose generalisations which apply across languages: cause-unspecified verbs alternate in all languages, while only some languages allow the alternation if the event is either externally or internally caused. To allow the alternation in the latter cases, languages need a special grammatical mechanism. In English, for example, this mechanism is not available, which is why only cause-unspecified verbs alternate. The alternation is thus blocked in both verbs describing externally caused and internally caused events.

Alexiadou's account is based not only on the observations about the availability of the alternation, but also about morphological encoding of the alternation across languages. Unlike English, which does not mark the alternation morphologically (note that the two versions of English verbs in (1-3) are morphologically identical), other languages encode the alternation in different ways, as shown in (3).

		Causative	Anticausative
	Mongolian	xajl-**uul**-ax	xajl-ax
		'melt'	'melt'
(3)	Russian	rasplavit	rasplavit-**sja**
		'melt'	'melt'
	Japanese	atum-**eru**	atum-**aru**
		'gather'	'gather'

An analysis of the distribution of morphological marking across languages leads Haspelmath (1993) to introduce the notion of likelihood into his account of the meaning of the alternating verbs. In a study of 31 verbs in 21 languages from all over the world, Haspelmath notices that certain verbs tend to get the same kind of marking across languages. For each verb, he calculates the ratio between the number of languages which mark the anticausative version and the number of languages which mark the causative version of the verb. He interprets this ratio as a quantitative measure of how spontaneous events described by the verbs are. As each verb is assigned a different score, ranking the verbs according to the score results in a "scale of increasing likelihood of spontaneous occurrence". Events with a low anticausative/causative ratio (e.g. *boil*, *dry*, *melt*) are likely to occur spontaneously, while events with a high ratio (e.g. *break*, *close*, *split*) are likely to be caused by an external causer.

3 The Model

Our study pursues the quantitative assessment of the likelihood of external causation in the events described the alternating verbs. We estimate the likelihood by means of a Bayesian model which divides events into classes based on the distribution of causative and anticausative uses of verbs in a corpus. By varying the settings of the model, we address two questions discussed in the linguistic literature: 1) Is the distinction between externally caused and internally caused events binary,, as argued by Levin and Rappaport Hovav (1994), or are there are intermediate classes, as argued by Alexiadou (2010)? and 2) Do we obtain better estimation of the likelihood from cross-linguistic than from monolingual data?

We design a probabilistic model which estimates the likelihood of external causation and generates a probability distribution over a given number of event classes for each verb in a given set of verbs. The model formalises the intuition that an externally caused event tends to be expressed by a verb in its causative realisation. In other words, if the likelihood of external causation of the event is encoded in the use of the verb which describes the event, then the causer is expected to appear frequently in the realisations of the verb. The opposite is expected for internally caused events. Cause-unspecified events are expected to appear with and without the causer equally.

To take into account the two questions discussed in the theoretical approaches, namely the number of classes and the role of cross-linguistic data in the classification of events, we design four versions of the model, varying the input data and the number of classes in the output: a) monolingual input and two classes; b) cross-linguistic input and two classes; c) monolingual input and three classes; d) cross-linguistic input and three classes.

The current cross-linguistic versions of the model include only two languages, English and German, because we test the models in a minimal cross-linguistic setting. In principle, the approach can be easily extended to include any number of languages.

As it can be seen in its graphical representation in Figure 1, the model consists of three variables in the monolingual version and of four variables in the cross-linguistic version.

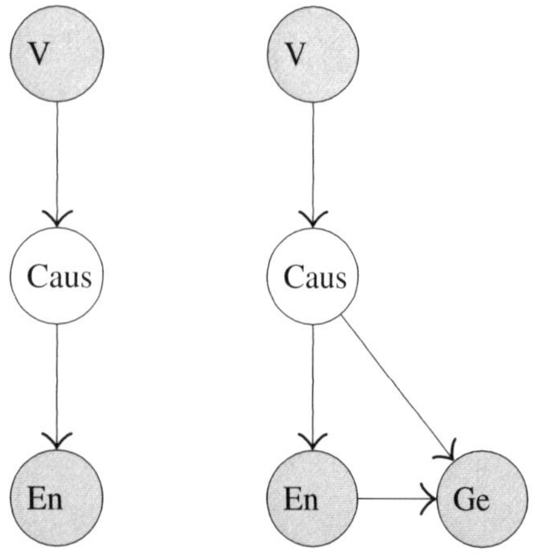

Figure 1: Two version of the Bayesian net model for estimating external causation.

The first variable in both versions is the set of verbs V. This can be any given set of verbs.

The second variable is the event class of the verb, for which we use the symbol $Caus$. The values of this variable depend on the assumed classification. In the two-class version, the values are *causative*, representing externally caused events, and *anticausative*, representing internally caused events. In the three-class version, the variable can take one more value, *unspecified*, representing cause-unspecified events.

The third (En) and the fourth (Ge) (in the cross-linguistic version) variables are the surface realisations of the verbs in parallel instances. These variables take three values: *causative* for active transitive use, *anticausative* for intransitive use, and *passive* for passive use in the languages in question.

We represent the relations between the variables as a Bayesian network. The variable that represents the event class of verbs ($Caus$) is unobserved. The values for the other three variables are observed in the data source. Note that the input to the model does not contain the information about the event class at any point.

The dependence between En and Ge in the bilingual version of the model represents the fact that the two instances of a verb are translations of each other, but does not represent the direction of translation in the actual data. The form of the instance in one language depends on the form of the parallel instance because they express the same meaning in the same context, regardless of the direction of translation.

Assuming that the variables are related as in Figure 1, En and Ge are conditionally independent of V given $Caus$, so we can calculate the probability of the model as in (4) for the monolingual version and as in (6) for the cross-linguistic version.

(4)
$$P(v, caus, en) = P(v) \cdot P(caus|v) \cdot P(en|caus)$$

(5)
$$P(caus|v, en) = \frac{P(v) \cdot P(caus|v) \cdot P(en|caus)}{\sum_{caus} P(v) \cdot P(caus|v) \cdot P(en|caus)}$$

We estimate the conditional probability of the event class given the verb ($P(caus|v)$) by querying the model, as shown in (5) for the monolingual version and in (7) for the bilingual version..

$$P(v, caus, en, ge) = P(v) \cdot P(caus|v) \cdot P(en|caus) \cdot P(ge|caus, en) \quad (6)$$

$$P(caus|v, en, ge) = \frac{P(v) \cdot P(caus|v) \cdot P(en|caus) \cdot P(ge|caus, en)}{\sum_{caus} P(v) \cdot P(caus|v) \cdot P(en|caus) \cdot P(ge|caus, en)} \quad (7)$$

We assign to each verb the event class that is most probable given the verb, as in (8).

$$caus\_class(verb) = arg\, max_{caus} P(caus|v) \quad (8)$$

All the variables in the model are defined so that the parameters can be estimated on the basis of frequencies of instances of verbs automatically extracted from parsed corpora.

4 Experiments

The accuracy of the predictions of the model is evaluated in experiments.

4.1 Materials and Methods

The verbs for which we estimate the likelihood are the 354 verbs that participate in the causative alternation in English, as listed by Levin (1993), and the 26 verbs listed as alternating in a typological study (Haspelmath, 1993).

We estimate the parameters of the model by implementing the expectation-maximisation algorithm. The algorithm is initialised by assigning different arbitrary values to the parameters of the model. The classification reported in the paper is obtained after 100 iterations.

We train the classifier using the data automatically extracted from an English-German parallel corpus (Europarl (Koehn, 2005)). Both monolingual and bilingual input data are extracted from the parallel corpus. All German verbs which are word-aligned with the alternating English verbs listed in the literature are regarded as German equivalents. By extracting cross-linguistic equivalents automatically from a parallel corpus, we avoid manual translation into German of the lists of English verbs discussed in the literature. In this way, we eliminate the judgements which would be involved in the process of translation.

The corpus is syntactically parsed (using the MaltParser (Nivre et al., 2007)) and word-aligned (using GIZA++ (Och and Ney, 2003)). For both the syntactic parses and word alignments, we reuse the data provided by Bouma et al. (2010).

We extract only the instances of verbs where both the object (if there is one) and the subject are realised in the same clause, excluding the instances involving syntactic movements and coreference. Transitive instances are considered causative realisations, intransitive anticausative. We count passive instances separately because they are formally transitive, but they usually do not express the causer.

German equivalents of English alternating verbs are extracted in two steps. First, all verbs occurring as transitive, intransitive, and passive were extracted from the German sentences that are sentence-aligned with the English sentences containing the instances of alternating verbs. These instances were considered candidate translations. The instances that are the translations of the English instances were then selected on the basis of word alignments. Instances where at least one element (the verb, the head of its object, or the head of its subject) is aligned with at least one element in the English instance were considered aligned.

Only the instances of English verbs that are translated with a corresponding finite verbal form in German are extracted, excluding the cases where English verbs are translated into a corresponding non-finite form such as infinitive, nominalization, or participle in German.

4.2 Evaluation

We evaluate the performance of the models against the scale of spontaneous occurrence proposed by Haspelmath (1993), shown in (9). We expect the verbs classified as internally caused by our models to correspond to the verbs with a low morphological anticausative/causative ratio (those on the left side of the scale). The opposite is expected for externally caused verbs. Cause-unspecified verbs are expected to be in the middle of Haspelmath's scale.

(9) *boil, dry, wake up, sink, learn-teach, melt, stop, turn, dissolve, burn, fill, finish, begin, spread, roll, develop, rise-raise, improve, rock, connect, change, gather, open, break, close, split*

To evaluate the output of our models against the scale, we discretise the scale so that the agreement is maximised for each version of the model. For example, the threshold which divides the verbs into anticausative and causative in the two-way classification is set after the verb *turn*.

By evaluating the performance of our models against a typology-based measure, we avoid eliciting human judgements, which is a known problem in computational approaches to causality. The downside of this approach is that such evaluation is currently possible for a relatively small number of verbs.

5 Results and Discussion

Table 1 shows all the confusion matrices of the classifications performed automatically in comparison with the classifications based on the typology rankings.[1]

In the two-way classification, the two versions of the model, with monolingual and with bilingual input, result in identical classifications. The agreement of the models with the typological ranking can be considered very good (85%). The optimal threshold divides the verbs into two asymmetric classes: eight verbs in the internally caused class and eighteen in the externally caused class. The agreement is better for the internally caused class.

In the three way-classification, the performance of both versions of the model drops. In this setting, the output of the two versions differs: there are two verbs which are classified as externally caused by the monolingual version and as cause-unspecified by the bilingual version, which results in a slightly better performance of the bilingual version. Given the small number of evaluated verbs, however, this tendency cannot be considered significant.

The three-way classification is more difficult than the two-way classification, but the difficulty is not only due to the number of classes, but also to the fact that two of the classes are not well-distinguished in the data. While the class of internally caused events is relatively easily distinguished (small number of errors in all classifications), the classes of externally caused and cause-unspecified verbs are hard to distinguish. This finding supports the two-way classification argued for in the literature.

The classification performed by the bilingual model indicates that the distinction between externally caused and cause-unspecified verbs might still exist. Compared to the monolingual classification, more verbs are classified as cause-unspecified, and they are grouped in the middle of the typological scale. Since the model takes into account cross-linguistic variation in the realisations of the alternating verbs, the observed difference in the performance could be interpreted as a sign that the distinction between cause-unspecified and externally caused events does emerge in cross-linguistic contexts.

While supporting the two-way classification of events, our experiments do not provide a definite answer to the question of whether there are more than two classes of events. To obtain significant results, more verbs need to be evaluated. However, the typological data used in our experiments (Haspelmath, 1993) are not easily available. This kind of data are currently not included in the typological resources (such as the WALS database (Dryer and Haspelmath, 2013)), but they can, in principle, be collected from other electronic sources of language documentation, which are increasingly available for many different languages.

6 Related Work

The proposed distinction between externally and internally caused events is addressed by McKoon and Macfarland (2000). They study twenty-one verbs defined in the linguistic literature as describing internally caused events and fourteen verbs describing externally caused events. Their corpus study shows that the appearance of these verbs as causative (transitive) and anticausative (intransitive) cannot be used as a diagnostic for the kind of meaning that has been attributed to them.

Since internally caused verbs do not enter the alternation, they were expected to be found in intransitive clauses only. This, however, was not the case. The probability for some of these verbs to occur in a transitive clause is actually quite high (0.63 for the verb *corrode*, for example). More importantly, no difference was found in the probability of the verbs denoting internally caused and externally caused events to occur as transitive or as intransitive. This means that the acceptability judgements used in the qualitative analysis do not apply to all the verbs in question, and, also, not to all the instances of these verbs.

[1] The table contains 26 instead of 31 verbs because corpus data could not be reliably extracted for some phrasal verbs listed by Haspelmath.

Model	2-class				3-class					
	Monolingual		Bilingual		Monolingual			Bilingual		
Typology	acaus	caus	acaus	caus	acaus	caus	unspec.	acaus	caus	unspec.
acaus	**8**	0	**8**	0	**6**	0	1	**6**	0	1
caus	4	**14**	4	**14**	0	**3**	0	0	**3**	0
unspec.	—	—	—	—	4	5	**7**	4	3	**9**
Agreement	85%		85%		61%			69%		

Table 1: Per class and overall agreement between the corpus-based and the typology-based classification of verbs; acaus = internally caused, caus = externally caused, unspec. = cause-unspecified.

Even though the most obvious prediction concerning the corpus instances of the two groups of verbs was not confirmed, the corpus data were still found to support the distinction between the two groups. Examining 50 randomly selected instances of transitive uses of each of the studied verbs, McKoon and Macfarland (2000) find that, when used in a transitive clause, internally caused change-of-state verbs tend to occur with a limited set of subjects, while externally caused verbs can occur with a wider range of subjects. This difference is statistically significant.

The relation between frequencies of certain uses and the lexical semantics of English verbs has been explored by Merlo and Stevenson (2001) in the context of automatic verb classification. Merlo and Stevenson (2001) show that information collected from instances of verbs in a corpus can be used to distinguish between three different classes which all include verbs that alternate between transitive and intransitive use. The classes in question are manner of motion verbs (10), which alternate only in a limited number of languages, externally caused change of state verbs (11), alternating across languages, and performance/creation verbs, which are not lexical causatives (12).

(10) a. The horse raced past the barn.
b. The jockey raced the horse past the barn.

(11) a. The butter melted in the pan.
b. The cook melted the butter in the pan.

(12) a. The boy played.
b. The boy played soccer.

One of the most useful features for the classification proved to be the *causativity* feature. It represents the fact that, in the causative alternation, the same lexical items can occur both as subjects and as objects of the same verb. This feature sets apart the two causative classes from the performance class.

In the context of psycholinguistic empirical approaches to encoding causality in verbs, it has been established that assigning a causal relation to a sequence of events can be influenced by the native languages (Wolff et al., 2009a; Wolff and Ventura, 2009b). English speakers, for instance, tend to assign causal relations more than Russian speakers.

In our study, we draw on the fact that the semantic properties of verbs are reflected in the way they are used in a corpus, established by the previous studies. We explore this relationship further, relating it to a deeper semantic analysis and to the typological distribution of grammatical features.

7 Conclusion and Future Work

The experiments presented in this article provide empirical evidence that contribute to a better understanding of the relationship between the causal semantics of verbs, their formal morphological and syntactic properties, and the variation in their use. We have shown that the likelihood of external causation of events is encoded in the distribution of the causative and anticausative uses of verbs. Two classes of events, externally caused and internally caused events, can be distinguished automatically based on corpus data.

In future work, we will further investigate the question of whether there are more than two classes of events and how they are distinguished. We will explore potential tendencies indicated by our findings. We will apply the approach proposed in this article to an extended data set. On one hand, we will collect typological data for more verbs, exploring possibilities of automatic data extraction. On the other hand, we will include more languages in the model to ensure a better representation of cross-linguistic variation.

References

Artemis Alexiadou, Elena Anagnostopoulou, and Florian Schfer. 2006. The properties of anticausatives crosslinguistically. In Mara Frascarelli, editor, *Phases of Interpretation*, pages 187–212, Berlin, New York. Mouton de Gruyter.

Artemis Alexiadou. 2010. On the morpho-syntax of (anti-)causative verbs. In Malka Rappaport Hovav, Edit Doron, and Ivy Sichel, editors, *Syntax, Lexical Semantics and Event Structure*, pages 177–203, Oxford. Oxford University Press.

Steven Bethard. 2007. *Finding Event, Temporal and Causal Structure in Text: A Machine Learning Approach*. Ph.D. thesis, University of Colorado at Boulder.

Gerlof Bouma, Lilja Øvrelid, and Jonas Kuhn. 2010. Towards a large parallel corpus of cleft constructions. In *Proceedings of the Seventh conference on International Language Resources and Evaluation (LREC'10)*, Valletta, Malta. European Language Resources Association.

Matthew S. Dryer and Martin Haspelmath, editors. 2013. *WALS Online*. Max Planck Institute for Evolutionary Anthropology, Leipzig.

Pascale Fung, Zhaojun Wu, Yongsheng Yang, and Dekai Wu. 2007. Learning bilingual semantic frames: Shallow semantic parsing vs. semantic role projection. In *11th Conference on Theoretical and Methodological Issues in Machine Translation (TMI 2007)*, pages 75–84, Skovde, Sweden.

Matthew Gerber and Joyce Y. Chai. 2012. Semantic role labeling of implicit arguments for nominal predicates. *Computational Linguistics*, 38(4):755–798.

Thomas Gilovich, Robert Vallone, and Amos Tversky. 1985. The hot hand in basketball: On the misperception of random sequences. *Cognitive Psychology*, 17(3):295–314.

Cécile Grivaz. 2012. *Automatic extraction of causal knowledge from natural language texts*. Ph.D. thesis, University of Geneva.

Martin Haspelmath. 1993. More on typology of inchoative/causative verb alternations. In Bernard Comrie and Maria Polinsky, editors, *Causatives and transitivity*, volume 23, pages 87–121, Amsterdam/Philadelphia. John Benjamins Publishing Co.

Karin Kipper Schuler. 2005. *VerbNet: A broad-coverage, comprehensive verb lexicon*. Ph.D. thesis, University of Pennsylvania.

Philipp Koehn. 2005. Europarl: A parallel corpus for statistical machine translation. In *Proceedings of MT Summit 2005*, Phuket, Thailand.

Mirella Lapata and Chris Brew. 2004. Verb class disambiguation using informative priors. *Computational Linguistics*, 30(1):45–73.

Beth Levin and Malka Rappaport Hovav. 1994. A preliminary analysis of causative verbs in English. *Lingua*, 92:35–77.

Beth Levin and Malka Rappaport Hovav. 2005. *Argument realization*. Cambridge University Press, Cambridge.

Beth Levin. 1993. *English verb classes and alternations : a preliminary investigation*. The University of Chicago Press, Chicago.

Lluís Màrquez, Xavier Carreras, Kenneth C. Litkowski, and Suzanne Stevenson. 2008. Semantic role labeling: An introduction to the special issue. *Computational Linguistics*, 34(2):145–159.

Gail McKoon and Talke Macfarland. 2000. Externally and internally caused change of state verbs. *Language*, 76(4):833–858.

Paola Merlo and Susanne Stevenson. 2001. Automatic verb classification based on statistical distribution of argument structure. *Computational Linguistics*, 27(3):373–408.

Albert Michotte. 1963. *The perception of causality*. Basic Books, Oxford, England.

Jacques Moeschler. 2011. Causal, inferential and temporal connectives: Why 'parce que' is the only causal connective in French. In S. Hancil, editor, *Marqueurs discursifs et subjectivité*, pages 97–114, Rouen. Presses Universitaires de Rouen et du Havre.

Joakim Nivre, Johan Hall, Jens Nilsson, Chanev Atanas, Gleşen Eryiğit, Sandra Kbler, Svetoslav Marinov, and Erwin Marsi. 2007. MaltParser: A language-independent system for data-driven dependency parsing. *Natural Language Engineering*, 13(2):95–135.

Franz Josef Och and Hermann Ney. 2003. A systematic comparison of various statistical alignment models. *Computational Linguistics*, 29(1):19–52.

Sebastian Padó and Mirella Lapata. 2009. Cross-lingual annotation projection of semantic roles. *Journal of Artificial Intelligence Research*, 36:307–340.

Martha Palmer, Daniel Gildea, and Paul Kingsbury. 2005. The Proposition Bank: An annotated corpus of semantic roles. *Computational Linguistics*, 31(1):71–105.

James Pustejovsky. 1995. *The generative lexicon*. MIT Press, Cambridge, MA.

Gillian Ramchand. 2008. *Verb Meaning and the Lexicon: A First Phase Syntax*. Cambridge Studies in Linguistics. Cambridge University Press, Cambridge.

Michael Roth and Anette Frank. 2012. Aligning predicate argument structures in monolingual comparable texts: A new corpus for a new task. In **SEM 2012: The First Joint Conference on Lexical and Computational Semantics – Volume 1: Proceedings of the main conference and the shared task, and Volume 2: Proceedings of the Sixth International Workshop on Semantic Evaluation (SemEval 2012)*, pages 218–227, Montréal, Canada, 7-8 June. Association for Computational Linguistics.

Florian Schafer. 2009. The causative alternation. In *Language and Linguistics Compass*, volume 3, pages 641–681. Blackwell Publishing.

Leonard Talmy. 2000. *Towards a cognitive semantics*. The MIT Press, Cambridge Mass.

Amos Tversky and Daniel Kahneman. 1982. Causal schemata in judgments under uncertainty. In Daniel Kahneman, Paul Slovic, and Amos Tversky, editors, *Judgement Under Uncertainty: Heuristics and Biases*.

Lonneke van der Plas, Paola Merlo, and James Henderson. 2011. Scaling up automatic cross-lingual semantic role annotation. In *Proceedings of the 49th Annual Meeting of the Association for Computational Linguistics: Human Language Technologies*, pages 299–304, Portland, Oregon, USA, June. Association for Computational Linguistics.

Phillip Wolff and Tatyana Ventura. 2009b. When Russians learn English: How the semantics of causation may change. *Bilingualism: Language and Cognition*, 12(2):153–176.

Phillip Wolff, Ga-Hyun Jeon, and Yu Li. 2009a. Causal agents in English, Korean and Chinese: The role of internal and external causation. *Language and Cognition*, 1(2):165–194.

Sandrine Zufferey. 2012. 'Car, parce que, puisque' revisited: Three empirical studies on French causal connectives. *Journal of Pragmatics*, 44:138–153.

Recognizing Causality in Verb-Noun Pairs via Noun and Verb Semantics

Mehwish Riaz and Roxana Girju
Department of Computer Science and Beckman Institute
University of Illinois at Urbana-Champaign
Urbana, IL 61801, USA
{mriaz2,girju}@illinois.edu

Abstract

Several supervised approaches have been proposed for causality identification by relying on shallow linguistic features. However, such features do not lead to improved performance. Therefore, novel sources of knowledge are required to achieve progress on this problem. In this paper, we propose a model for the recognition of causality in verb-noun pairs by employing additional types of knowledge along with linguistic features. In particular, we focus on identifying and employing semantic classes of nouns and verbs with high tendency to encode cause or non-cause relations. Our model incorporates the information about these classes to minimize errors in predictions made by a basic supervised classifier relying merely on shallow linguistic features. As compared with this basic classifier our model achieves 14.74% (29.57%) improvement in F-score (accuracy), respectively.

1 Introduction

The automatic detection of causal relations is important for various natural language processing applications such as question answering, text summarization, text understanding and event prediction. Causality can be expressed using various natural language constructions (Girju and Moldovan, 2002; Chang and Choi, 2006). Consider the following examples where causal relations are encoded using (1) a verb-verb pair, (2) a noun-noun pair and (3) a verb-noun pair.

1. Five shoppers were **killed** when a car **blew up** at an outdoor market.
2. The attack on Kirkuk's police intelligence complex sees further **deaths** after **violence** spilled over a nearby shopping mall.
3. At least 1,833 people **died** in **hurricane**.

Since, the task of automatic recognition of causality is quite challenging, researchers have addressed this problem by considering specific constructions. For example, various models have been proposed to identify causation between verbs (Bethard and Martin, 2008; Beamer and Girju, 2009; Riaz and Girju, 2010; Do et al., 2011; Riaz and Girju, 2013) and between nouns (Girju and Moldovan, 2002; Girju, 2003). Do et al. (2011) have worked with verb-noun pairs for causality detection but they focused only on a small list of predefined nouns representing events.

In this paper, we focus on the task of identifying causality encoded by verb-noun pairs (example 3). We propose a novel model which first predicts cause or non-cause relations using a supervised classifier and then incorporates additional types of knowledge to reduce errors in predictions. Using a supervised classifier, our model identifies causation by employing shallow linguistic features (e.g., lemmas of verb and noun, words between verb and noun). Such features have been used successfully for various NLP tasks (e.g., part-of-speech tagging, named entity recognition, etc.) but confinement to such features does not help much to achieve performance for identifying causation (Riaz and Girju, 2013). Therefore, in our model we plug in additional types of knowledge to obtain better predictions for the current task. For example, we identify the semantic classes of nouns and verbs with high tendency to encode cause or non-causal relations and use this knowledge to achieve better performance. Specifically, the contributions of this paper are as follows:

- In order to build a supervised classifier, we use the annotations of FrameNet to generate a training corpus of verb-noun instances encoding cause and non-cause relations. We propose a set of linguistic features to learn and identify causal relations.

- In order to make intelligent predictions, it is important for our model to have knowledge about the semantic classes of nouns with high tendency to encode causal or non-causal relations. For example, a named entity such as person, organization or location may have high tendency to encode non-causality unless a metonymic reading is associated with it. In our approach, we identify such semantic classes of nouns by exploiting a named entity recognizer, the annotations of frame elements provided in FrameNet and WordNet.
- Verbs are the important components of language for expressing events of various types. For example, Pustejovsky et al. (2003) have classified events into eight semantic classes: OCCURRENCE, PERCEPTION, REPORTING, ASPECTUAL, STATE, I_STATE, I_ACTION and MODAL. We argue that there are some semantic classes in this list with high tendency to encode cause or non-cause relations. For example, reporting events represented by verbs say, tell, etc., have high tendency to just report other events instead of encoding causality with them. In our model, we use such information to reduce errors in predictions.
- Each causal relation is characterized by two roles i.e., cause and its effect. In example 3 above, the noun "hurricane" is cause and the verb "died" is its effect. However, a verb-noun pair may not encode causality when a verb and a noun represent same event. For example, in instance "Colin Powell **presented** further evidence in his **presentation**.", the verb "presented" and the noun "presentation" represent same event of "presenting" and thus encoding non-cause relation with each other. In our model, we determine the verb-noun pairs representing same or distinct events to make predictions accordingly.
- We adopt the framework of Integer Linear Programming (ILP) (Roth and Yih, 2004; Do et al., 2011) to combine all the above types of knowledge for the current task.

This paper is organized as follows. In next section, we briefly review the previous research done for identifying causality. We introduce our model and evaluation with discussion on results in section 3 and 4, respectively. The section 5 of the paper concludes our current research.

2 Related Work

In computational linguistics, researchers have always shown interest in the task of automatic recognition of causal relations because success on this task is critical for various natural language applications (Girju, 2003; Chklovski and Pantel, 2004; Radinsky and Horvitz, 2013).

Following the successful employment of linguistic features for various tasks (e.g., part-of-speech tagging, named entity recognition, etc.), initially NLP researchers proposed approaches relying mainly on such features to identify causality (Girju, 2003; Bethard and Martin, 2008; Sporleder and Lascarides, 2008; Pitler and Nenkova, 2009; Pitler et al., 2009). However, researchers have recently shifted their attention from these features and tried to consider other sources of knowledge for extracting causal relations (Beamer and Girju, 2009; Riaz and Girju, 2010; Do et al., 2011; Riaz and Girju, 2013). For example, Riaz and Girju (2010) and Do et al. (2011) have proposed unsupervised metrics for learning causal dependencies between two events. Do et al. (2011) have also incorporated minimal supervision with unsupervised metrics. For a pair of events (a, b), their model makes the decision of cause or non-cause relation based on unsupervised co-occurrence counts and then improves this decision by using minimal supervision from the causal and non-causal discourse markers (e.g., because, although, etc.).

In search of novel and effective types of knowledge to identify causation between two verbal events, Riaz and Girju (2013) have proposed a model to learn a Knowledge Base (KB_c) of verb-verb pairs. In this knowledge base, the English language verb-verb pairs are automatically classified into three categories: (1) Strongly Causal, (2) Ambiguous and (2) Strongly Non-Causal. The Strongly Causal and Strongly Non-Causal categories contain verb-verb pairs with highest and least tendency to encode causality, respectively and rest of the verb-verb pairs are considered ambiguous with tendency to encode both types of relations. They claim that this knowledge base of verb-verb pairs is a rich source of causal associations. The incorporation of this resource into a causality detection model can help identifying causality with better performance. In this research, we also try to go beyond the scope of shallow linguistic features and identify additional interesting types of knowledge for the current task.

3 Computational Model for Identifying Causality

In this section, we introduce our model for identifying causality encoded by verb-noun pairs. Specifically, we extract all main verbs and noun phrases from a sentence and predict cause or non-cause relation on verb-noun_phrase (v-np) pairs. In order to make task easier, we consider only those v-np pairs where v (verb) is grammatically connected to np (noun phrase). We assume that a v and np are grammatically connected if there exists a dependency relation between them in the dependency tree. We apply a dependency parser (Marneffe et al., 2006) to identify such dependencies. Our model first employs a supervised classifier relying on linguistic features to make binary predictions (i.e., does a verb-noun_phrase pair encode a cause or non-cause relation?). We then incorporate additional types of knowledge on top of these binary predictions to improve performance.

3.1 Supervised Classifier

In this section, we propose a basic supervised classifier to identify causation encoded by v-np pairs. To set up this supervised classifier, we need a training corpus of instances of v-np pairs encoding cause and non-cause relations. For this purpose, we employ the annotations of FrameNet project (Baker et al., 1998) provided for verbs. For example, consider the following annotation from FrameNet for the verb "dying" with argument "solvent abuse" where the pair "dying-solvent abuse" encodes causality.

> A campaign has started to try to cut the rising number of children **dying** [$_{cause}$ from **solvent abuse**].

To generate a training corpus, we collect annotations of verbs from FrameNet s.t. the annotated element (aka. frame element) is a noun phrase. For example, we get a causal training instance of "dying-solvent abuse" pair from the above annotation. We assume that if a FrameNet's annotated element contains a verb in it then this may not represent a training instance of v-np pair. For example, we do not consider the following annotation in our training corpus where causality is encoded between two verbs i.e., "died-fell".

> A fitness fanatic **died** [$_{cause}$ when 26 stone of weights **fell** on him as he exercised].

After extracting training instances from FrameNet, we assign them cause (c) and non-cause (¬ c) labels. We manually examined the inventory of labels of FrameNet and use the following scheme to assign the c or $\neg c$ to each training instance. All the annotations of FrameNet with following labels are considered as causal training instances and rest of the annotations are considered as non-causal training instances.

> Purpose, Internal cause, Result, External cause, Cause, Reason, Explanation, Required situation, Purpose of Event, Negative consequences, resulting action, Effect, Cause of shine, Purpose of Goods, Response action, Enabled situation, Grinding cause, Trigger

For this work, we have acquired $2,158$ $(65,777)$ cause (non-cause) training instances from FrameNet. Since, the non-cause instances are very large in number, our supervised model tends to assign non-cause labels to almost all instances. Therefore, we employ equal number of cause and non-cause instances for training. In future, we plan to extract more annotations from the FrameNet and employ more than one human annotators to assign the labels of cause and non-cause relations to the full inventory of labels of FrameNet.

- **Lexical Features:** verb, lemma of verb, noun phrase, lemma of all words of noun phrase, head noun of noun phrase, lemmas of all words between verb and head noun of noun phrase.
- **Semantic Features:** We adopted this feature from Girju (2003) to capture the semantics of nouns. The 9 noun hierarchies of WordNet i.e., entity, psychological feature, abstraction, state, event, act, group, possession, phenomenon are used as this feature. Each of these hierarchies is set to 1 if any sense of the head noun of noun phrase lies in that hierarchy otherwise set to 0.
- **Structural Features:** This feature is applied by considering both subject (i.e., sub_in_np) and object (i.e., obj_in_np) of a verb. For example, for a v-np pair the variable sub_in_np is set to 1 if the subject of v is contained in np, set to 0 if the subject of v is not contained in np and set to -1 if the subject of v is not available in the instance. The subject and object of a verb are its core arguments and may sometime be part of an event represented by a verb. Therefore, these argument may have high tendency to encode non-cause relations.

We set up the following integer linear program after acquiring predictions of c and ¬ c labels using our supervised classifier.

$$Z_1 = \max \sum_{\text{v-np} \in I} \sum_{l \in L_1} x_1(\text{v-np}, l) P(\text{v-np}, l) \quad (1)$$

$$\sum_{l \in L_1} x_1(\text{v-np}, l) = 1 \quad \forall \, \text{v-np} \in I \quad (2)$$

$$x_1(\text{v-np}, l) \in \{0, 1\} \quad \forall \, \text{v-np} \in I \quad \forall l \in L_1 \quad (3)$$

Here $L_1 = \{c, \neg c\}$, I is the set of all instances of v-np pairs and $x_1(\text{v-np}, l)$ is the decision variable set to 1 only if the label $l \in L_1$ is assigned to v-np. The Equation 2 constraints that only one label out of $|L_1|$ choices can be assigned to a v-np pair. The equation 3 requires $x_1(\text{v-np}, l)$ to be a binary variable. Specifically, we try to maximize the objective function Z_1 (equation 1) which assigns the label cause or non-cause to all v-np pairs (i.e., set the variables $x_1(\text{v-np}, l)$ to 1 or 0 for all $l \in L_1$ and for all v-np pairs in I) depending on the probabilities of assignment of labels (i.e., $P(\text{v-np}, l))$[1]. These probabilities can be obtained by running a supervised classification algorithm (e.g., Naive Bayes and Maximum Entropy). In our experiments, we provide results using the following probabilities acquired with Naive Bayes.

$$\begin{aligned} P(\text{v-np}, c) &= 1.0 - \frac{\sum_{k=1}^{n} logP(f_k \mid c)}{\sum_{k=1}^{n} \sum_{l \in (c, \neg c)} logP(f_k \mid l)} \\ P(\text{v-np}, \neg c) &= 1.0 - P((v, np), c) \end{aligned} \quad (4)$$

where f_k is a feature, n is total number of features and $P(f_k \mid l)$ is the smoothed probability of a feature f_k given the training instances of label l.

3.2 Knowledge of Semantic classes of nouns

Philospher Jaegwon Kim (Kim, 1993) (as cited by Girju and Moldovan (2002)) pointed out that the entities which represent either causes or effects are often events, but also conditions, states, phenomena, processes, and sometimes even facts. Therefore, according to this our model should have knowledge of the semantic classes of noun phrases with high tendency to encode cause or non-cause relations. Considering this type of knowledge, we can automatically review and correct the wrong predictions made by our basic supervised classifier.

[1] We use the integer linear program solver available at http://sourceforge.net/projects/lpsolve/

We argue that if a noun phrase represents a named entity then it can have least tendency to encode causal relations unless there is a metonymic reading associated with it. For example, consider the following cause and non-cause examples where noun phrase is a named entity.

4. Sandy **hit Cuba** as a Category 3 hurricane.
5. Almost all the weapon sites in Iraq were **destroyed** by the **United States**.

In example 4, Cuba is location and does not encode causality. However, in example 5 the pair "destroyed-the United States" encode causality where a metonymic reading is associated with the location. We apply Named Entity Recognizer (Finkel et al., 2005) and assume if a noun phrase is identified as a named entity then its corresponding verb-noun_phrase pair encodes non-cause relation. This constraint can lead to a false negative prediction when the metonymic reading is associated with a noun phrase. In order to avoid as much false negatives as possible, we imply the following simple rule i.e., if one of the following cue words appear between a verb and a noun phrase then do not apply the constraint stated above.

by, from, because of, through, for

In our experiments, the above simple rule helps avoiding some false negatives but in future any subsequent improvement with a better metonomy resolver (Markert and Nissim, 2009) should improve the performance of our model.

In addition to named entities, there can be various noun phrases with least tendency to encode causation. Consider the following example, where "city" is a location and does not encode cause-effect relation with the verb "remained".

> Substantially fewer people **remained** in the **city** during the Hurricane Ivan evacuation.

In this work, we identify the semantic classes of noun phrases which do not normally represent events, conditions, states, phenomena, processes and thus have high tendency to encode non-cause relations. For this purpose, we manually examine the inventory of labels assigned to noun phrases in FrameNet (see table 1) and classify these labels into two classes (c_np and $\neg c_{np}$). Here, the class c_{np} ($\neg c_{np}$) represents the labels of noun phrases with high (less) tendency to encode cause-effect relations. For example, the label "Place" $\in \neg c_{np}$

(see table 1) represents a location and it may have least tendency to encode causality if metonymy is not associated with it. Using the classification of frame elements in table 1, we obtain the annotations of noun phrases from FrameNet and categorize these annotations into c_{np} and $\neg c_{np}$ classes. On top of the annotations of these two semantic classes, we build a supervised classifier for predicting c_{np} or $\neg c_{np}$ label for the noun phrases. After obtaining predictions, we select all noun phrases lying in class $\neg c_{np}$ and apply the same constraint stated above for the named entities. We use the following set of features to set up a supervised classifier for c_{np} and $\neg c_{np}$ labels.

- **Lexical Features:** words of noun phrase, lemmas of all words of noun phrase, head word of noun phrase, first two (three) (four) letters of head noun of noun phrase, last two, (three) (four) letters of head noun of noun phrase.
- **Word Class Features:** part-of-speech tags of all words of noun phrase, part-of-speech tag of head noun of noun phrase.
- **Semantic Features:** all (frequent) sense(s) of head noun of noun phrase.

We have acquired 23,334 (81,279) training instances of c_{np} ($\neg c_{np}$) class, respectively for this work. We also use WordNet to obtain more training instances of these classes. We follow the approach similar to Girju and Moldovan (2002) and adopt some senses of WordNet (shown in table 1) to acquire training instances of noun phrases. For example, considering the table 1, we assign $\neg c_{np}$ label to any noun whose all senses in WordNet lie in the semantic hierarchy originated by the sense {time period, period of time, period}. Following this scheme, we extract instances of nouns and noun phrases from English GigaWord corpus and assign the labels c_{np} and $\neg c_{np}$ to them by employing WordNet senses given in table 1. Girju and Moldovan (2002) have used similar scheme to rank noun phrases according to their tendency to encode causation. In comparison to them, we use the WordNet senses to increase the size of our training set of noun phrases obtained using FrameNet above. In addition to this, we build a automatic classifier on the training data obtained using labels of FrameNet and WordNet senses to classify noun phrases of test instances into two semantics classes (i.e., c_{np} and $\neg c_{np}$). In our training corpus of there are $2,214,68$ instances of noun phrases (50% belongs to each of c_{np} and $\neg c_{np}$ classes).

We incorporate the knowledge of semantics of nouns in our model by making the following additions to the integer linear program introduced in section 3.1.

$$Z_2 = Z_1 + \sum_{\text{np:v-np} \in I} \sum_{l \in L_2} x_2(\text{np}, l) P(\text{np}, l) \quad (5)$$

$$\sum_{l \in L_2} x_2(\text{np}, l) = 1 \quad \forall \, \text{np} : \text{v-np} \in I - M \quad (6)$$

$$x_2(\text{np}, l) \in \{0, 1\} \quad \forall \, \text{np} : \text{v-np} \in I - M \quad \forall l \in L_2 \quad (7)$$

$$x_1(\text{v-np}, \neg c) - x_2(\text{np}, \neg c_{np}) \geq 0 \quad \forall \, \text{np} : \text{v-np}, \quad \forall \, \text{v-np} \in I - M \quad (8)$$

Here $L_2 = \{c_{np}, \neg c_{np}\}$ and M is the set of instances of those v-np pairs for which we consider the possibility of attachment of metonymic reading with np, $x_2(\text{np}, l)$ is the decision variable set to 1 only if the label $l \in L_2$ is assigned to np. The Equation 6 constraints that only one label out of $|L_2|$ choices can be assigned to a np. The equation 7 requires $x_2(\text{np}, l)$ to be a binary variable. The constraint 8 assumes that if an np belongs to the semantic class $\neg c_{np}$ then its corresponding pair v-np is assigned the label $\neg c$. We maximize the objective function Z_2 (equation 5) of our integer linear program subject to the constraints introduced above. We predict the semantic class of a noun phrase using the supervised classifier for c_{np} and $\neg c_{np}$ classes and set the probabilities i.e., $P(\text{np}, l) = 1, P(\text{np}, \{L_2\} - \{l\}) = 0$ if the label $l \in L_2$ is assigned to np. Again we use Naive Bayes to predict the labels for noun phrases. Also before running this supervised classifier, we run the named entity recognizer and assign $\neg c_{np}$ labels to all noun phrases identified as named entities. For our model, we apply named entity recognizer for seven classes i.e., LOCATION, PERSON, ORGANIZATION, DATE, TIME, MONEY, PERCENT (Finkel et al., 2005).

3.3 Knowledge of Semantic classes of verbs

In this section, we introduce our method to incorporate the knowledge of semantic classes of verbs to identify causation. Verbs are the components of language for expressing events of various types. In TimeBank corpus, Pustejovsky et al. (2003) have introduced eight semantic classes of events i.e., OCCURRENCE, PERCEPTION, REPORTING, ASPECTUAL, STATE, I_STATE, I_ACTION and MODAL. According to the definitions of these classes provided by Pustejovsky

Semantic Class	FrameNet Labels	WordNet Senses
c_{np}	Event, Goal, Purpose, Cause, Internal cause, External cause, Result, Means, Reason, Phenomena	{act, deed, human action, human activity}, {phenomenon}, {state}, {psychological feature}, {event}, {causal agent, cause, causal agency}
$\neg c_{np}$	Artist, Performer, Duration, Time, Place, Distributor, Area, Path, Direction, Sub-region	{time period, period of time, period}, {measure, quantity, amount}, {group, grouping}, {organization, organisation}, {time unit, unit of time}, {clock time, time}

Table 1: This table presents some examples of FrameNet labels in c_{np} and $\neg c_{np}$ classes. The full set of labels in both semantic classes are given in appendix A. It also presents the WordNet senses of nouns lying in c_{np} and $\neg c_{np}$ classes.

et al. (2003), the reporting events describe the action of a person, declare something or narrate an event e.g., the reporting events represented by verbs say, tell, etc. Here, we argue that a reporting event has the least tendency to encode causation because such an event only describes or narrates another event instead of encoding causality with it. We assume that the verbs representing reporting events have least tendency to encode causation and thus their corresponding v-np pairs have least tendency to encode causation. To add this knowledge to our model, we consider two classes of verbs i.e., c_v and $\neg c_v$ where the class c_v ($\neg c_v$) contains the verbs with high (less) tendency to encode causation. Using above argument we claim that all verbs representing reporting events belong $\neg c_v$ class and verbs representing rest of the types of events belong to c_v class. We build a supervised classifier which automatically classifies verbs into c_v and $\neg c_v$ classes. We extract the instances of verbal events (i.e., verbs or verbal phrases) from TimeBank corpus and assign the labels c_v and $\neg c_v$ to these instances. Using these labeled instances, we build a supervised classifier by adopting the same set features as introduced in Bethard and Martin (2006) to identify semantic classes of verbs. Due to space constraint, we refer the reader to Bethard and Martin (2006) for the details of features. Again we use Naive Bayes to take predictions of c_v and $\neg c_v$ labels and their corresponding probabilities using equation 4.

We incorporate the knowledge of semantics of verbs in our model by making the following additions to the integer linear program.

$$Z_3 = Z_2 + \sum_{\text{v:v-np} \in I} \sum_{l \in L_3} x_3(\text{v}, l) P(\text{v}, l) \quad (9)$$

$$\sum_{l \in L_3} x_3(\text{v}, l) = 1 \quad \forall \text{v : v-np} \in I \quad (10)$$

$$x_3(\text{v}, l) \in \{0, 1\} \quad \forall \text{v : v-np} \in I \quad \forall l \in L_3 \quad (11)$$

$$x_1(\text{v-np}, \neg c) - x_3(\text{v}, \neg c_v) >= 0 \quad (12)$$
$$\forall \text{v : v-np}, \quad \forall \text{v-np} \in I$$

$$x_3(\text{v}, c_v) - x_1(\text{v-np}, c) >= 0 \quad (13)$$
$$\forall \text{v : v-np}, \quad \forall \text{v-np} \in I$$

Here $L_3 = \{c_v, \neg c_v\}$, $x_3(\text{v}, l)$ is the decision variable set to 1 only if the label $l \in L_3$ is assigned to v. The Equation 10 constraints that only one label out of $|L_3|$ choices can be assigned to a v. The equation 11 requires $x_3(\text{v}, l)$ to be a binary variable. The constraint 12 assumes if a verb v belongs to the class c_v (i.e., has least potential to encode causation) then its corresponding pair v-np encodes non-causality. The constraint 12 enforces that if a verb v belongs to the class $\neg c_v$ then its corresponding v-np pair is assigned the label $\neg c$. Similarly, the constraint 16 enforces that if a v-np pair encodes causality then its verb v has potential to encode causal relation. We maximize the objective function Z_3 subject to the constraints introduced above.

3.4 Knowledge of Indistinguishable Verb and Noun

As introduced earlier, each causal relation is characterized by two roles i.e., cause and its effect. In order to encode causal relation, two components of an instance of verb-noun_phrase pair need to represent distinct events, processes or phenomena. Employing simple lexical matching, we determine if a verb and a noun phrase represent same event or not as follows:

- We use NOMLEX (Macleod et al., 2009) to transform a verb into its corresponding nominalization and use the following text segments for lexical matching.
  T_v = [Subject] verb [Object][2]
  T_n = Head noun of noun phrase
- We remove stopwords and duplicate words from T_v and T_n and take lemmas of all words. If the subject or object or both arguments are contained in noun phrase then we remove these arguments from T_v. We determine the probability of a verb (v) and a noun phrase (np) representing same event as follows. If head noun (i.e., T_n) lexically matches with any word of T_v then set P(v $\equiv$ np) to 1 and 0 otherwise.

We assign non-cause relation if P(v $\equiv$ np) = 1. Next, we incorporate the knowledge of indistinguishable verb and noun in our model using the following additions to our integer linear program.

$$Z_4 = Z_3 + \sum_{\text{v-np} \in I} \sum_{l \in L_4} x_4(\text{v-np}, l) P(\text{v-np}, l) \quad (14)$$

$$\sum_{l \in L_4} x_4(\text{v-np}, l) = 1 \quad \forall \, \text{v-np} \in I \quad (15)$$

$$x_4(\text{v-np}, l) \in \{0, 1\} \quad \forall \, \text{v-np} \in I, \forall l \in L_4$$

$$x_1(\text{v-np}, \neg c) - x_4(\text{v-np}, \equiv) \geq 0 \quad \forall \, \text{v-np} \in I \quad (16)$$

Here $L_4 = \{\equiv, \not\equiv\}$ where the label $\equiv$ ($\not\equiv$) represents same (distinct) events, $x_4(\text{v-np}, l)$ is the decision variable set to 1 only if the label $l \in L_4$ is assigned to v-np. The Equation 15 constraints that only one label out of $|L_4|$ choices can be assigned to a v-np pair. The equation 16 requires $x_4(\text{v-np}, l)$ to be a binary variable. The constraint 16 enforces that if a v-np pair belongs to the class $\equiv$ then this pair is assigned the label $\neg c$. We maximize the objective function Z_4 subject to the constraints introduced above.

4 Evaluation and Discussion

In this section we present the experiments, evaluation procedures, and a discussion on the results achieved through our model for the current task.

In order to evaluate our model, we generated a test set with instances of form verb-noun_phrase where the verb is grammatically connected to the noun phrase in an instance. For this purpose, we collected three wiki articles on the topics of Hurricane Katrina, Iraq War and Egyptian Revolution of 2011. We selected first 100 sentences from these articles and applied part-of-speech tagger (Toutanova et al., 2003) and dependency parser (Marneffe et al., 2006) on these sentences. Using each sentence, we extracted all verb-noun_phrase pairs where the verb has a dependency relation with any word of noun phrase. We manually inspected all of the extracted instances and removed those instances in which a word had been wrongly classified as a verb by the part-of-speech tagger. There are total 1106 instances in our test set. We assigned the task of annotation of these instances with cause and non-cause relations to a human annotator. Using manipulation theory of causality (Woodward, 2008), we adopted the annotation guidelines from Riaz and Girju (2010) which is as follows: "Assign cause label to a pair (**a**, **b**), if the following two conditions are satisfied: (1), **a** temporally precedes/overlap **b** in time, (2) while keeping as many state of affairs constant as possible, modifying **a** must entail predictably modifying **b**. Otherwise assign non-cause label. "

We have 149 (957) cause (non-cause) instances in our test set[3], respectively. We evaluate the performance of our model using F-score and accuracy evaluation measures (see table 2 for results).

The results in table 2 reveal that the basic supervised classifier is a naive model and achieves only 27.27% F-score and 46.47% accuracy. The addition of novel types of knowledge introduced in section 3 (i.e., the model Basic+SCN$_M$+SCV+IVN) brings 14.74% (29.57%) improvements in F-score (accuracy), respectively. These results show that the knowledge of semantics of nouns and verbs and the knowledge of indistinguishable verb and noun are critical to achieve performance. The maximum improvement in results is achieved with the addition of semantic classes of nouns (i.e., Basic+SCN$_M$). The consideration of association of metonymic readings using model Basic+SCN$_M$ helps us to maintain recall as compared with SCN$_{!M}$ and therefore brings better F-score.

One can notice that almost all models suffer from low precision which leads to lower F-scores. Although, our model achieves 14.58% increase in precision over basic supervised classifier, the lack of high precision is still responsible for lower F-

[2]Following Riaz ang Girju (2010), we assume that the subject and object of a verb are parts of an event represented by a verb. Therefore, we use these arguments along with a verb for lexical matching with a noun phrase.

[3]We will make the test set available

Model	Basic	+SCN$_{!M}$	+SCN$_M$	+SCN$_M$+SCV	+SCN$_M$+SCV+IVN
Accuracy	46.47	75.76	74.41	75.31	76.04
Precision	16.69	28.14	29.53	30.47	31.27
Recall	74.49	50.66	64.00	64.00	64.00
F-score	27.27	39.19	40.42	41.29	42.01

Table 2: This table presents results of the basic supervised classifier (i.e., Basic) and the models after incrementally adding the knowledge of semantic classes of nouns without consideration of metonymic readings (i.e., + SCN$_{!M}$), the knowledge of semantic classes of nouns with consideration of metonymic readings (i.e., + SCN$_M$), the knowledge of semantic classes of verbs (i.e., +SCN$_M$+SCV) and the knowledge of indistinguishable verb and noun (i.e., +SCN$_M$+SCV+IVN).

score. The highly skewed distribution of test set with only 13.47% causal instances results in lots of false positives. We manually examined false positives to determine the language features which may help us reducing more false positives without affecting F-score. We noticed that the direct objects of the verbs are mostly part of the event represented by the verbs and therefore encodes non-causation with the verbs. For example, consider following instances:

6. The hurricane surge protection failures prompted a lawsuit.
7. They provided weather forecasts.

In example 6, "lawsuit" is the direct object of the verb "prompted" and is part of the event represented by the verb "prompt". However there is a cause relation between "protection failures" and "prompted". Similarly in example 7, the direct object "forecasts" is part of the "providing" event and thus the noun phrase "weather forecasts" encode non-cause relation with the verb "provide". Therefore, following this observation we employed the training corpus of cause and non-cause relations (see section 3.1) and learned the structure of verb-noun_phrase pairs encoding non-cause relations most of the time. We considered only those training instances where the subject and/or object of the verb was available. For the current purpose, we picked up following four features (1) sub_in_np, (2) !sub_in_np, (3) obj_in_np and (4) !obj_in_np. Just to remind the reader, the feature sub_in_np (!sub_in_np) is set to 1 if the subject of the verb is (not) contained in the noun phrase np, respectively. For each of the above four features, the percentage of cause and entropy of relations with that feature are as follows:

- sub_in_np (%c = 34.72, Entropy = 0.931)
- !sub_in_np (%c = 59.71, Entropy = 0.972)
- obj_in_np (%c = 28.89, Entropy = 0.867)
- !obj_in_np (%c = 55.30, Entropy = 0.991).

There are two important observations from above scores: (1) verbs mostly encode non-cause relations with their objects and subjects (i.e., high $\%\neg c$ with obj_in_np and sub_in_np), (2) among obj_in_np and sub_in_np features, obj_in_np yields least entropy i.e., there are least chances of encoding causality of a verb with its object.

Considering the above statistics, we enforce the constraint on each verb-noun_phrase pair that if the object of the verb is contained in the noun phrase of the above pair then assigns non-cause relation to that pair. Using this constraint, we obtain 46.61% (80.74%) F-score (accuracy), respectively. This confirms our observation that the object of a verb is normally part of an event represented by the verb and thus it encodes non-cause relation with the verb.

In this research, we have utilized novel types of knowledge to improve the performance of our model. In future, we need to consider more additional information (e.g., predictions from metonymy resolver) to achieve further progress.

5 Conclusion

In this paper, we have proposed a model for identifying causality in verb-noun pairs by employing the knowledge of semantic classes of nouns and verbs and the knowledge of indistinguishable noun and verb of an instance along with shallow linguistic features. Our empirical evaluation of model has revealed that such novel types of knowledge are critical to achieve a better performance on the current task. Following the encouraging results achieved by our model, we invite researchers to investigate more interesting types of knowledge in future to make further progress on the task of recognizing causality.

References

Collin F. Baker, Charles J. Fillmore and John B. Lowe. 1998. The Berkeley FrameNet project. *In proceedings of the Association for Computational Linguistics and International Conference on Computational Linguistics (COLING-ACL).*

Brandon Beamer and Roxana Girju. 2009. Using a Bigram Event Model to Predict Causal Potential. *In proceedings of the Conference on Computational Linguistics and intelligent Text Processing (CICLING).*

Steven Bethard and James H. Martin. 2006. Identification of Event Mentions and their Semantic Class. *In Proceedings of the Conference on Empirical Methods in Natural Language Processing (EMNLP).*

Steven Bethard and James H. Martin. 2008. Learning Semantic Links from a Corpus of Parallel Temporal and Causal Relations. *In proceedings of the Association for Computational Linguistics (ACL).*

Du-Seong Chang and Key-Sun Choi. 2006. Incremental cue phrase learning and bootstrapping method for causality extraction using cue phrase and word pair probabilities. *Information Processing and Management, volume 42 issue 3, 662678.*

Timothy Chklovski and Patrick Pantel. 2004. VerbOcean: Mining the Web for Fine-Grained Semantic Verb Relations. *In proceedings of the Conference on Empirical Methods in Natural Language Processing (EMNLP).*

Quang X. Do, Yee S. Chen and Dan Roth. 2011. Minimally Supervised Event Causality Identication. *In proceedings of the Conference on Empirical Methods in Natural Language Processing (EMNLP).*

Jenny R. Finkel, Trond Grenager, and Christopher Manning. 2005. Incorporating Non-local Information into Information Extraction Systems by Gibbs Sampling. *In Proceedings of the Association for Computational Linguistics (ACL).*

Roxana Girju. 2003. Automatic detection of causal relations for Question Answering. *Association for Computational Linguistics ACL, Workshop on Multilingual Summarization and Question Answering Machine Learning and Beyond.*

Roxana Girju and Dan Moldovan. 2002. Mining Answers for Causation Questions. *In American Associations of Artificial Intelligence (AAAI), 2002 Symposium.*

Jaegwon Kim. 1993. Causes and Events. Mackie on Causation. *In Cansation, Oxford Readings in Philosophy, ed. Ernest Sosa, and Michael Tooley, Oxford University Press.*

Catherine Macleod, Ralph Grishman, Adam Meyers, Leslie Barrett, Ruth Reeves. 1998. NOMLEX: A Lexicon of Nominalizations. *In proceedings of EURALEX.*

Katja Markert, Malvina Nissim 2009. Data and models for metonymy resolution. *Language Resources and Evaluation Volume 43 Issue 2, Pages 123−138.*

Marie-Catherine de Marneffe, Bill MacCartney and Christopher D. Manning. 2006. Generating typed dependency parses from phrase structure parses. *In Proceedings of the International Conference on Language Resources and Evaluation (LREC).*

Emily Pitler, Annie Louis and Ani Nenkova. 2009. Automatic Sense Prediction for Implicit Discourse Relations in Text. *In proceedings of ACL-IJCNLP.*

Emily Pitler and Ani Nenkova. 2009. Using Syntax to Disambiguate Explicit Discourse Connectives in Text. *In proceedings of ACL-IJCNLP.*

James Pustejovsky, Patrick Hanks, Roser Saur, Andrew See, Robert Gaizauskas, Andrea Setzer, Dragomir Radev, Beth Sundheim, David Day, Lisa Ferro and Marcia Lazo. 2003. The TIMEBANK Corpus. *In Proceedings of Corpus Linguistics.*

Kira Radinsky and Eric Horvitz. 2013. Mining the Web to Predict Future Events. *In proceedings of sixth ACM international conference on Web search and data mining, (WSDM).*

Mehwish Riaz and Roxana Girju. 2010. Another Look at Causality: Discovering Scenario-Specific Contingency Relationships with No Supervision. *In proceedings of the IEEE 4th International Conference on Semantic Computing (ICSC).*

Mehwish Riaz and Roxana Girju 2013. Toward a Better Understanding of Causality between Verbal Events: Extraction and Analysis of the Causal Power of Verb-Verb Associations. *Proceedings of the annual SIGdial Meeting on Discourse and Dialogue (SIGDIAL).*

Dan Roth and Wen-tau Yih 2004. A Linear Programming Formulation for Global Inference in Natural Language Tasks. *In Proceedings of the Annual Conference on Computational Natural Language Learning (CoNLL).*

Caroline Sporleder and Alex Lascarides. 2008. Using automatically labelled examples to classify rhetorical relations: An assessment. *Journal of Natural Language Engineering Volume 14 Issue 3.*

Kristina Toutanova, Dan Klein, Christopher Manning, and Yoram Singer. 2003. Feature-Rich Part-of-Speech Tagging with a Cyclic Dependency Network. *In Proceedings of Human Language Technology and North American Chapter of the Association for Computational Linguistics (HLT-NAACL).*

James Woodward. 2008. Causation and Manipulation. *Online Encyclopedia of Philosophy.*

Appendix A. Semantic Classes of Nouns

This appendix presents the FrameNet labels we assign to c_{np} and $\neg c_{np}$ classes (see section 3.2).

Semantic Class	FrameNet Labels
c_{np}	Event, Goal, Purpose, Cause, Internal cause, External cause, Result, Means, Reason, Phenomena, Characterization, Coordinated event, Final state, Information, Topic, Containing event, Mental content, Action, Experience, Impactee, Impactor, Message, Question, Circumstances, Desired goal, Explanation, Required situation, Complaint, Content, Activity, Intended goal, Phenomenon, State, Dependent state, Forgery, Purpose of Event, Negative consequences, Inference, Appraisal, Noisy event, Function, Evidence, Process, Paradigm, Standard, Old order, Focal occasion, Landmark occasion, resulting action, Victim, Issue, Effect, State of affairs, Cause of shine, Qualification, Undesirable Event, Skill, Precept, Outcome, Norm, Act, State of Affairs, Phenomenon 1, Phenomenon 2, Quality Eventuality, Expression, Intended event, Cognate event, Epistemic stance, Goal conditions, Possession, Support Proposition, Domain of Relevance, Charges, Idea, Initial subevent, Hypothetical event, Scene, Purpose of Goods, Response action, Motivation, Executed, Affliction, Medication, Treatment, Stimulus, Last subevent, Undesirable situation, Sleep state, Initial state, Enabled situation, Grinding cause, Finding, Case, Legal Basis, Role of focal participant, Trigger, Authenticity, World state, Emotion, Emotional state, Evaluation, New idea, Production, Performance, Undertaking, Destination event
$\neg c_{np}$	Artist, Performer, Duration, Time, Place, Distributor, Area, Path, Direction, Sub-region, Creator, Copy, Original, Iteration, Manner, Frequency, Agent, Body part, Depictive, Theme, Subregion, Area, Degree, Angle, Fixed location, Path shape, Addressee, Entity, Individual 1, Individual 2, Road, Distance, Speaker, Medium, Clothing, Wearer, Bodypart of agent, Locus, Cognizer, Salient entity, Name, Inspector, Ground, Unwanted entity, Location of inspector, Researcher, Population, Searcher, Sought entity, Instrument, Created entity, Components, Forgoer, Desirable, Bad entity, Dodger, Experiencer, Vehicle, Self mover, Speed, Cotheme, Consecutive, Re encoding, Supplier, Individuals, Driver, Complainer, Communicator, Protagonist, Attribute, Final value, Item, Initial value, Difference, Group, Value range, Co participant, Perceiver agentive, Target symbol, Location of perceiver, Location, Expected entity, Focal participant, Time of Event, Variable, Limits, Limit1, Limit2, Point of contact, Goods, Lessee, Lessor, Money, Rate, Unit, Reversive, Perceiver passive, Sound, Sound source, Location of source, Fidelity, Official, Selector, Role, Concessive, New leader, Body, Old leader, Leader, Governed, Result size, Size change, Dimension, Initial size, Elapsed time, Interval, Category, Criteria, Text, Final correlate, Correlate, Initial correlate, Manipulator, Side 1, Sides, Side 2, Perpetrator, Value 1, Value 2, Actor, Partner 2, Partner 1, Partners, Figure, Resident, Co resident, Student, Subject, Institution, Level, Teacher, Undergoer, Subregion bodypart, Course, Owner, Defendant, Judge, Co abductee, Location of appearance, Material, Accused, Arraign authority, Hair, Configuration, Emitter, Beam, Amount of progress, Evaluee, Patient, Buyer, Seller, Recipient, Relay, Relative location, Connector, Items, Part 1, Part 2, Parts, Whole, Name source, Payer, Fine, Executioner, Interlocutor 1, Interlocutor 2, Interlocutors, Healer, Food, Cook, Container, Heating instrument, Temperature setting, Resource controller, Resource, Donor, Constant location, Carrier, Sender, Co theme, Transport means, Holding location, Rope, Knot, Handle, Containing object, Fastener, Enclosed region, Container portal, Aggregate, Suspect, Authorities, Offense, Source of legal authority, Ingestor, Ingestibles, Sleeper, Pieces, Goal area, Period of iterations, Mode of transportation, Produced food, Ingredients, Cognizer agent, Excreter, Excreta, Air, Perceptual source, Escapee, Undesirable location, Evader, Capture, Pursuer, Amount of discussion, Means of communication, Periodicity, Author, Honoree, Reader, Child, Mother, Father, Egg, Flammables, Flame, Kindler, Mass theme, Address, Intermediary, Communication, Location of communicator, Firearm, Indicated entity, Hearer, Sub region, Member, Object, Organization, Guardian, New Status, Arguer, Criterion, Liquid, Impactors, Force, Coparticipant, Holding Location, Legal basis, Precipitation, Quantity, Voice, Duration of endstate, Period of Iterations, Employer, Employee, Task, Position, Compensation, Field, Place of employment, Amount of work, Contract basis, Recipients, Hot Cold source, Temperature goal, Temperature change, Hot/Cold source, Dryee, Temperature, Traveler, Iterations, Baggage, Deformer, Resistant surface, Fluid, Injured Party, Avenger, Injury, Punishment, Offender, Grinder, Profiled item, Standard item, Profiled attribute, Standard attribute, Extent, Source emitter, Emission, Sub source, Item 1, Item 2, Parameter, Form, Chosen, Change agent, Injuring entity, Severity, Substance, Delivery device, Entry path, Wrong, Amends, Grounds, Expressor, Basis, Signs, Manufacturer, Product, Factory, Consumer, Interested party, Performer1, Performer2, Whole patient, Destroyer, Exporting area, Importing area, Accuracy, Time of Eventuality, Indicator, Indicated, Audience, Valued entity, Journey, Duration of end state, Killer, Beneficiary, Destination time, Landmark time, Seat of emotion, Arguers, Arguer1, Arguer2, Company, Asset, Origin, Sound maker, Static object, Themes, Heat source, Following distance, Perceiver, Intended perceiver, Location of expressor, Path of gaze, Relatives, Final temperature, Particular iteration, Participant 1, Language

Table 3: This table presents the FrameNet labels we assign to c_{np} and $\neg c_{np}$ classes.

Author Index